TOR BUS
REMEMBERED

by Roger Grimley

Cover photograph:
This AEC Reliance was unique in that it had more red than was usual in the "Tor Bus" livery. The main places served were painted in gold lettering along the side of the roof. It is seen here in Liverton village (R. Marshall)

IBSN No. 1 872863 07 8

Published by Kithead Ltd in conjunction with Roger Grimley
at De Salis Drive, Hampton Lovett, Droitwich Spa, Worcs, WR9 0QE

Preface

"If one must go to Widecombe, let it be in spring or autumn, for in winter the chances are weighted too heavily in favour of freezing cold, snow or blinding mist; and in high summer it is thronged with sightseers". For many people a trip to Widecombe involved a ride on the "Tor Bus", for Dartmoor and the "Tor Bus" were inseparable. Leaving the busy streets of Newton Abbot, it traversed the Bovey Basin, with its clay pits, to reach the foothills of Dartmoor and a steep climb through the woods to Ilsington, with low gear engaged and horn sounding a warning of approach. Then on to the impressive rocks of Haytor and the open road over the moorland. Soon Widecombe-in-the-Moor could be seen below, beautifully situated in its broad green valley, forming a green oasis amid the rocky heights and barren moors. Then the final steep descent, with low gear engaged and the driver controlling the brakes continuously, into Widecombe village where the bus terminated under the trees overlooked by the Parish Church, the "Cathedral of the Moor".

From a small horse drawn wagonette, the Potter family progressed to a motor-lorry fitted with benches on market days, then to purpose-built buses. From a village shop and some rented land at Liverton the business grew to a garage, workshops and filling station serving motorists as well as the firm's own buses, taxis and lorries. The early vehicles, when packed with folk coming home from market, would steam to a halt on the steep hills. The able bodied would walk to the top and wait for the bus to recover and proceed on its way. Then, in later years, modern underfloor-engined vehicles appeared, always smartly turned out in the maroon, red and black livery with no exterior advertisements other than the company's name and title.

The service catered for local people, day visitors to the moors, those staying at local hotels as well as those following "Uncle Tom Cobley" to Widecombe Fair. Although the combined population of the main villages was only about 2,000 a daily service was maintained.

The "Tor Bus" is remembered with much affection as a family business which served the travelling public for over forty years. It was part of the social life of the area, carrying people from all classes of society. If you wanted to hear any local news or gossip then this was the place to go. "I heard it on Potter's bus" was said every day when parishioners were telling each other of local gossip or their exploits. No one was ever knowingly left behind – "Where's Mrs So-and-So, we'd better hang on for her". At busy times there was always space for another passenger and in the bad weather so prevalent on Dartmoor great efforts were made to keep running. How apt were the mottoes of the firm – "Never leave anyone behind", "Always room for one more" and "We'll get through".

Acknowledgements

Thanks are due to many people for their help and assistance. First must be Bob Cornish, whose enthusiasm for and interest in the "Tor Bus" was a constant source of inspiration. He has worked tirelessly to unearth contacts, arrange meetings and play host. Without him this book would not have been possible.

Special thanks to Mr Leslie Manley. His unique knowledge and information, coupled with a clear memory, has been of tremendous assistance. It was a joy to sit and listen to his reminiscences and this book owes much to his willingness to talk and patience with the listeners. Also to Fred Pady, long time member of the staff of J. Potter & Sons and a marvellous contributor of memories of times long ago.

Muriel Bunclark, Bill Baty, Jean and Bill Blinston, Roger and Sue Retallick, Denis Tyler and Dick Wills have all made special contributions, for which grateful thanks. Geoff Bruce, Bob Crawley, Les Folkard, John Madge, Mike Parsons and the P.S.V. Circle have all made their records available. Photographs are from Alan Broughall, Alan B. Cross, Roy Marshall, Roy Sambourne, the collection of Bob Cornish and local sources in the Ilsington area, to all of whom thanks are due.

Also my love and gratitude to Barbara Grimley. Not only has she been of great practical help in libraries, record offices and throughout the highways and byways of Devon for many years but also she has been patient and encouraging.

Last of all, if any reader can add to this record then the author would be delighted to hear from them.

Roger Grimley

Coddington
May, 1994

Chapter One : The Early Years

A Wednesday morning in January and on Dartmoor the mist was thick and freezing. The cattle and ponies stood cold and miserable, sheep clustered together along the edges of the moorland road. Snow lay on the moor. On the steep hill up from Widecombe-in-the-Moor a low roar could be heard in the distance. Gradually it came closer and closer until, eventually, a shadowy outline could be seen through the damp, cold curtain of fog. The dark shape drew closer and it could be identified as a maroon, red and black bus. After reaching the brow of the hill, Potter's "Tor Bus" squeezed through the narrow White Gate and crawled along the moorland road, before eventually turning right and dropping down through Ilsington, then out of the mists and into Liverton.

In was in Liverton that John Potter had lived since about 1896. He was a Methodist lay preacher and in Mary Jane Easterbrook of Exbourne he found a good wife and partner, for she was a woman of determination. At first they lived in a cottage which had been part of the old Dame School before a new school building was erected at Blackpool, later moving to another cottage in Treacle Lane. They had a large family of whom three, George, Sidney and Wilfred play a part in this story.

John Potter, who had many skills including thatching and ditching, worked on local farms and undertook bark-ripping on coppice land at Ilsington for the Newton Abbot tanneries. He kept a few pigs and some bees. Prior to 1914 he had been employed at Stover Golf Club but on the outbreak of war this job finished. He did more thatching and ditching and he and Mary Jane bought more sows, then a cow, and then another cow. They were offered and took up the tenancy of the village bakery shop in Liverton and while a local house, Rora, was being rebuilt the craftsmen employed on it lodged with the Potters. The navvies working on the extension of the Ilsington water main from Liverton to Blackpool school were also accommodated. Gradually they built up their various enterprises.

Their first experience of passenger transport came when John and Mary Jane purchased a low wagonette which was mainly used to convey people to and from the railway stations at Heathfield and Bovey Tracey. At this time anyone wishing to go to and from Newton Abbot at a reasonable cost would ride on one of the horse-drawn wagons which ran two days each week. These were owned mainly by local farmers such as Thomas Hatch of Mill Farm, Liverton or Samuel Carpenter of Sanctuary, Ilsington. William Cooper, a hardware merchant at Coldeast, also ran a similar conveyance. By 1920 John Potter's original small vehicle had been changed for a larger wagonette and this was used not only for the station trips and private hire but also to compete with the other wagons on the regular runs to and from Newton on Wednesdays for market or on Saturdays for shopping. People would select the owner they wished to ride with. Some would chose John Potter because he was Chapel and Liberal. Others would prefer Samuel Carpenter who, being a farmer, was a Tory. They would sit two-up beside the driver, the rest behind amid baskets of eggs and other produce. Gradually the other owners retired or concentrated on other aspects of their business and John Potter was left as the main operator.

During 1920-21 the number of people travelling increased considerably. It became a problem to cope with the numbers wishing to travel to and from the station, to Newton Abbot or on a private party outings to Dartmoor and Becky Falls. The local Parish Council was agitating for a motor service and there was talk of the Great Western Railway Road Motors being operated from Bovey Tracey to Haytor, Widecombe, Becky Falls and Manaton. It was clear that something had to be done.

Motor transport was booming as men who had served in the Great War used the mechanical knowledge gained during their service and the money from their gratuities to buy surplus War Department vehicles which were being sold at Slough. However, although some tried them, these were too big and cumbersome for the narrow roads and steep hills of Dartmoor.

John Potter's sons were keen to have a motor. Sidney had worked as a caddy at Stover Golf Club before the war and there had talked to the chauffeurs of some of the prominent local people who were early motor-car owners. John Potter's sister had gone into service in London and married a man who was chauffeur to a Judge and so Sidney also developed a great interest in motors. John Potter, on the other hand, remembered the day at the turn of the century when an early motor vehicle was brought to Devon to be tried on the Dartmoor hills. It had started from Torquay one morning and come out through Newton Abbot and Liverton. As it got to the hill on the old road up to Ilsington village some people ran up and told the villagers of its coming. Everyone rushed out to see the spectacle and among them were two young men who worked on the same farm – John Potter and his friend William Honeywell. John had vowed that such a contraption would never catch on but now, years later, his own boys were urging him to buy one.

However, there were other factors to take into account. Because of the various enterprises in which the Potters were involved there were numerous visitors to the house and shop in Liverton. Among them was Thomas Lewis Beare, like John Potter a Chapel man. His family owned the foundry at Liverton and in years past they had been interested in the plan to build an alternative railway line between Exeter and Plymouth, avoiding the section around the coast which was liable to flood and storm damage. It was to have run via Chudleigh, Heathfield, Bickington and Ashburton to Totnes and would have helped Beare's foundry business. However, nothing became of it and so the family first rented, then bought, land on the marshes at Newton Abbot from the Earl of Devon and moved their business there lock, stock and barrel. They retained the land and property at Liverton and this was let for use as a pottery but the business was not successful. In 1921 Mr Beare met a Mr Hope, an

American whose family had moved from Staffordshire to the U.S.A. where they re-established themselves as potters. Mr Hope had returned to England, married and now wished to start a pottery. They were in discussion about a lease on the Liverton premises and Mr Beare could see that it would be advantageous for Mr Hope to be able to hire a motor vehicle to transport his products to and from the railway stations. There would also be regular haulage work for the Potter family. Before the Great War both Sidney and Wilfred Potter had been employed at Bovey Pottery, so they were familiar with that trade.

During 1920-21 Wilfred Potter worked for a syndicate that was boring locally for lignite. His job was to drive the horse and cart which carried the cores to the railway station for despatch to the testing stations. There were plans for a considerable business if the tests were positive and this could have been another source of work for a motor vehicle. In the event nothing came of the scheme but it added to the argument.

John Potter was not entirely convinced that to change to motor traction was a good idea. He thought that it was ridiculous to believe that motors could do better than horses and Mary Jane was concerned about spending so much of their hard earned money on such a contraption.

Mr A. Bulpin of Newton Abbot now came on the scene. His family owned a garage in Newton Abbot and he was involved in the Newton Abbot Touring Co., which ran the "Pride of the Moor" chars-a-banc from that town. He told the Potter family about the lighter, more suitable Model "T" Ford which was currently available. With mounting pressure from the three sons, George, Sidney and Wilfred, it was decided that an order should be placed for a motor which would replace the horse-drawn wagonette and could also be used to carry the Liverton Pottery products for Mr Hope. Tucker's Excelsior Garage in Bovey Tracey were approached to build a body but they did not consider that they had sufficient expertise. However, Vallance, the wheelwright in Kingsteignton, took on the job and produced an open, wooden-sided body to fit onto the Ford chassis. When necessary, benches could be fitted for passengers to sit on, with covers attached. The vehicle was painted dark red and black, colours that were to be familiar in the area for over forty years, and on the 7th July, 1921 it was registered TA 1706.

On Wednesdays and Saturdays passengers were conveyed to and from Newton Abbot. There was no fixed time table, the service ran according to demand. Two passengers rode in the cab with the driver, while the rest sat in the back of the open lorry. To have braved the elements on this vehicle, travelling on badly surfaced roads, must have been for those with a strong constitution. On other days it was used either to convey the pottery products or for general haulage.

A blow to the family was the death in 1921 of George Potter at the age of thirty-six. He had suffered from ill health, possibly as a result of his time working in the arsenic chambers at the Owlacombe Tin Mines at Sigford. He had married and moved to Newton Abbot where he had an insurance book but the intention was that he should have been the driver of the new motor. His passing left two of his brothers, Sidney and Wilfred, involved in the business with their parents.

Ownership of the vehicle brought an opportunity for the Potter family to travel. It was decided that when a number of relatives were visiting, there should be a day's outing to the parish of Exbourne, whence Mary Jane originated. Then on to the Okehampton area to see her brothers and the part of the county John Potter came from. Their first paid employee, thirteen year old Leslie Manley, was invited to join them.

The benches were fitted in the lorry and covered by potato sacks tied on with binder cord "to soften the ride". Off the party set, jiggedy-jig through Brimley and Bovey Tracey, with people running out to see them. Then on through the two hundred and eighty bends on the Moretonhampstead road. Suddenly out dashed a sheep dog from a farmyard. Sidney Potter, driving, put the brakes on and there was a big shake up as everyone on board, the food baskets, lemonade and cold tea, all went flying. The potato sacks had slipped and they all ended up in a heap, except little Leslie Manley. On starting, his mother had put Granfer Manley's old Candy coats in his potato sack and fixed them with leather belts from a dress basket. They held fast, so he kept his seat. Everyone brushed themselves off and sat down once more, then away again through Moretonhampstead – with more people running out to see them. At Easton Cross there was a different sort of horse-drawn conveyance than the Liverton people had been used to. It was a large char-a-banc drawn by two horses. The passengers were on holiday from London, staying at the Moor Park Hotel, Chagford, on a trip to Fingle Bridge and Gorge. They stopped for a talk and to let the lorry-bus cool down. When it was time to go, one man stood at the head of the horses while the other sat up with reins and whip. Sidney Potter turned the handle to start the motor, then away again.

They drove around Exbourne, seeing where uncles, aunts and cousins lived, before going on to Okehampton to visit Mary Jane Potter's brothers. Here they saw a fine motor car and Sidney was able to talk to the chauffeur. He later recalled that he thought the owner was a Mr Simmons, a well known benefactor in Okehampton. They then headed home, arriving back tired but happy with the freedom the new motor had given them.

Once the vehicle was in service it soon became apparent that it had been a good idea to turn to motor traction. Traffic exceeded expectations even though there was some competition for passengers from the Ashburton motor bus proprietors, who ran through Widecombe, Haytor, Ilsington and Liverton to Newton Abbot on market days. Those with goods to be carried found the lorry faster than horse and cart, and passengers were excited by the prospect of being able to see new places. The benches were regularly fitted to the vehicle for the carriage of people.

An early outing was that to celebrate the Chapel Anniversary. It was decided to take one lot of people to Teignmouth, then come back for more. Unfortunately, as the vehicle went up Ware Hill, near Kingsteignton, the pins

8

securing the seating came out and everyone slid back. However, all was taken in good part and it was an enjoyable day.

When planning the route for the new motor on its Wednesday and Saturday runs to Newton Abbot, various requests were received. To meet these it was decided to operate from Ilsington, through the lanes to Higher and Lower Brimley and into Bovey Tracey. Then to cut back to Liverton, past Cummins Cross and on to the "turnpike road" (A38 - Exeter to Plymouth main road), over Drumbridge cross roads and up the slope to Granite Lodge. This stop would serve people living in Teigngrace and Chudleigh Knighton as well as the inhabitants of Heathfield itself. In those days the latter consisted of Carbon Cottages and three or four other dwellings to the east of the lodge. The bus then turned and went back down to Drumbridge and followed the main Bovey Tracey road into Newton Abbot.

However, the narrow lanes around Brimley proved to be unsuitable for the vehicle and so, after a while, the service was altered to run from Smokey Cottages, Ilsington through the village and straight down to Liverton to resume the previous route. In due course there was a further alteration when instead of turning at Granite Lodge, Heathfield and returning to Drumbridge, the bus continued through Teigngrace village and past the Teign Bridge turning to join the main road just outside Newton Abbot.

Another early route was that between Newton Abbot and Combeinteignhead. Two of John Potter's sisters lived in the village and it was probably thought that the local connection would help business. However, there was strong competition from the "Newtonian" service run by Balls Ltd, of Newton Abbot which ran through Combeinteignhead on their service to and from Shaldon. This eventually proved too much and Potters withdrew.

In 1924 it was felt that the existing system of storing fuel at Potter's Liverton premises should be changed. Until then cans of petrol had been stacked on shelves in a building that had once been part of the bakery. The lorry-bus was kept in an open shed on the premises, which adjoined the old baker's shop run by Mary Jane Potter. A petrol storage tank was now installed and the vehicle was filled from a hand operated pump. The passenger operations were now an important part of the family business and the title "Potter's Bus Service" was used.

Although the Ashburton motor bus proprietors no longer ran through Ilsington and Liverton on their way to Newton market, there was another competitor. This was the "Speedwell" bus, owned by Messrs Howe and Turner of Kingsteignton, and running between Bovey Tracey and Newton Abbot. Journeys were routed via Brimley to Cummings Cross, thence to Drumbridge, a double-run to Granite Lodge, Heathfield, and on to Newton. Thus they competed with John Potter's bus over quite a length of its route. In 1925 they sold out to Babington of Ashburton (Blue Cars), one of those who had run through Liverton in 1921. Within a short while he, too, was taken over, selling to Devon General, and the section of route directly competing with Potters had been dropped.

9

Sidney Potter maintained his keen interest in automobiles and in 1926 he and his brother Wilfred visited a motor show. Here they saw a Dodge chassis fitted with a purpose-built fourteen-seater bus body. They were much taken with it and got into discussion with the manufacturer's representative. When he saw that they were interested it was suggested that they should buy it. Between them they had only five pounds in cash but the company was happy to accept this as a deposit and take the rest on trust. They took the bus and drove it back to Devon, their arrival home with the vehicle leaving their father somewhat aghast for there had been no thought of purchasing a new bus. Here it was registered TT 7388 on 23rd March, 1926.

The first problem was garaging as the new acquisition would not fit under the open shed used to house the Model "T" Ford lorry-bus. Considerable changes had to be made to an adjoining building, which had been the showroom for Beare's foundry in years past. Heath Bros, Builders were called in to demolish a wall alongside the road, then raise the roof and lower the floor level. The wall had housed a lions head water outlet which had originally fed the foundry and was the water supply for neighbouring cottages until 1914. Its source was a deep well up in the hills. The floor, which was lowered by about a foot, had consisted of Candy's first 1874 paving brick. These alterations enabled the Dodge to be "stabled".

At the request of Mr Sam Courtier of Haytor the route was now extended from Smokey Cottages, Ilsington to Haytor and, in addition, buses ran every day of the week. On Wednesdays and Saturdays there were four return journeys between Haytor and Newton, with a late extra from Newton Abbot back to Liverton. On the other weekdays there were three return trips; on Sundays two, increased to three in summer. In winter the level was reduced to one more appropriate for the season when there were no visitors to be conveyed to the moors, just locals to and from town. The business was now J. Potter & Sons and the title "Tor Bus" was adopted.

The family were again saddened by a death when in June, 1926, Mrs Mary Jane Potter passed away at the age of 68. She was a woman of courage and determination who had played an active role in many of the family enterprises and had carefully watched over the family finances.

With the Liverton Pottery working, some people from the Stoke-on-Trent area came down to Devon for employment. During the Staffordshire Pottery holiday weeks some of their friends and relations visited Devon to see them, camping at Liverton where a large house had been turned into flats to house pottery workers. When going in and out of Newton Abbot they would walk to Cummins Cross to ride on the "Tor Bus". Being used to the much larger vehicles operated in the urban areas of their homeland by companies such as the Potteries Electric Traction Co. Ltd they considered Potters' Dodge to be very small and it was promptly christened "the pigeon basket".

With the original Model "T" Ford lorry-bus now six years old it was decided to purchase another purpose-built bus in the spring of 1927. In view of the trust placed in the two Potter brothers by the Dodge representative in the previous year another vehicle of that make was bought. UO 1659 was, like its companion, a fourteen seater and arrived in March. The two buses maintained a pattern of operation in which the service level between Haytor and Newton Abbot varied with the season.

For these early buses the steep hills on the "Tor Bus" route were a considerable challenge. In the summer the heat caused the radiators to boil and all the able-bodied passengers would dismount and walk to the top of the hill, while the vehicle recovered and was eventually able to stagger to the top and re-load before continuing on its way. Where the gradient was just too much, the bus would be turned around and reversed up the slope – this being the lowest of the gears.

Winter brought the problems of ice and snow and this could result in some hair-raising moments for both driver and passengers. As one long time member of staff, Fred Pady, recalled about his experiences in later years - "I was going forward but the bus was going backward".

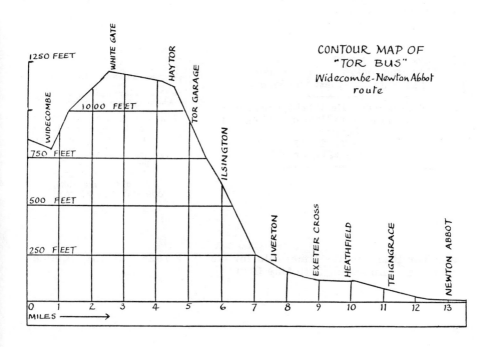

CONTOUR MAP OF
"TOR BUS"
Widecombe - Newton Abbot
route

The TOR BUS SERVICE
HAYTOR AND NEWTON ABBOT.
(via Ilsington and Liverton).

	Leave Haytor.	Leave Newton.
Monday, ...	9.30 ..	11.30
Tuesday, ...	1.30 ..	2.30
Thursday, ...	5.10 ..	6.10
Friday, ...		
Wednesdays and Saturdays	9.0* ..	10.0*
	1.30 ..	12.20
	3.45 ..	2.30
	6.10 ..	5.0
	8.15§ ..	7.15‡
	.. ..	10.0§
Sundays,	1.5 ..	2.15
	5.30 ..	9.0

*Liverton only on Wednesday
§ Sat. only.   ‡ last bus Wed.

For Teigngrace and Heathfield passengers
allow 35 minutes from Haytor to Granite
Lodge.
FULL JOURNEY, 2/3 RETURN.
J. POTTER and SONS.

TOR BUS SERVICE
NEWTON, HAYTOR, WIDECOMBE.

SUMMER TIME-TABLE,
Commencing MAY 27th, 1928.

MONDAY, TUESDAY, THURSDAY, FRIDAY.

Leave WIDECOMBE.	Leave HAYTOR.	Leave NEWTON.
	9-30	W 10-30
	11-0	12-0
1-15	1-30	W 2-30
4-15	5-0	W 6-15
7-15	8-0	9-0

WEDNESDAYS AND SATURDAYS.

No service to Widecombe WEDS. and SATS.		
	*9-30	*10-30
	11-0	12-20
	1-30	2-30
	3-15	5-0
	6-10	7-15
	8-15	9-10
		S10-30

SUNDAYS.

	10-30	W 11-30
1-15	1-30	W 2-30
5-15	5-30	W 6-30
7-15	8-0	9-0

* Leaves Haytor 9 a.m. and Newton 10-15 a.m. Wednesdays.
S Saturdays only.
W goes through to Widecombe.

The Management cannot accept any
responsibility for loss or delay on journey.

TOR 'BUS SERVICE, NEWTON—HAYTOR DAILY, Winter and Summer.
FIRST CLASS OPEN AND CLOSED CARS FOR HIRE.
'Phone : Haytor 33.
  ,, Bickington 9.
Wire : "TORBUS, HAYTOR."
J. POTTER and SONS,
TOR GARAGE, HAYTOR.

Left: Tor Bus Service timetable for October 1926. Right: summer timetable commencing 27th May 1928.

Chapter Two : To Widecombe-in-the-Moor

The year 1928 brought another development in the "Tor Bus" service. On Easter Monday special journeys were advertised, leaving Newton Abbot at 10.45 a.m. and 2 p.m. These followed the existing route to Liverton, Ilsington and Haytor but then continued over the high, open moorland road past Haytor Rocks and Rippon Tor, through White Gate and down the steep descent of Northway Hill into Widecombe, a popular place with visitors to Dartmoor. When the summer time table was introduced on 27th May, Widecombe was served five days each week, the exceptions being Wednesdays and Saturdays when the two buses were fully occupied with village traffic.

In those days some farmers would use a pony and trap to travel to market but for many the bus was the usual means of travel to the nearest market town. Dick Wills of Narracombe Farm, Ilsington remembers being sent down to the end of the lane as a small boy, nine or ten years old, to stop the bus and tell the driver to wait for his father, sometimes on a Wednesday morning when he was going to market. He would come running down the road, doing up his boot laces and buttoning up his gaiters as he came. The bus would be full of farmers and their wives going to Newton with their baskets of eggs, butter, cream, sacks of potatoes and all other farm produce, sometimes some ducks, fowls and chicken, some alive, some dead.

Newton Abbot was particularly lively on Wednesdays with thousands of people from all over the district congregated; large sums of money were paid over as cattle, dairy produce and a variety of other commodities changed hands. Farmers and their wives jostled with shoppers as people, vehicles and livestock crowded the streets and market. On Saturdays, when most people worked until midday, afternoon buses would be packed with those going off to Newton to see the sights and lights of town and to have some welcome light relief after a week of hard toil.

The buses also conveyed laundry baskets between the large houses at Haytor and a washer lady near Cummins Cross. They would be brought down on the first bus on Monday morning and returned on the dinner-time bus. Laundry was also conveyed to and from Newton Abbot.

The Potter business now included buses, taxis and lorries and to hold the growing fleet John, Sidney and Wilfred Potter decided that they ought to have premises of their own at which they could cater for the needs of motorists as well as their own vehicles. A field just above Smokey Cross, on the Ilsington –Haytor road, was purchased from the owner of Pinchaford Farm. On this the "Tor Garage" was erected. This provided garage space as well as being a public petrol filling station.   Beside it, bungalows were built for the two brothers. John Potter remained at the Liverton premises, which were still used.

On exactly the same day in 1926 that the first purpose-built Dodge bus was registered in the name of John Potter, another inhabitant of the parish had put a similar vehicle on the road.   He was John Dart, who ran a garage situated on the hill out of Ilsington towards Haytor.   His Dodge was named the "Haytor Coach" and was used for excursions from the village and for private party outings.   In 1928 he decided to run regularly to and from Newton Abbot market and commencing 25th April he began to compete with the "Tor Bus" for passengers from Widecombe and Haytor into Newton Abbot.   Some of his journeys also served the hamlet of Bagtor which was not covered by the Potter service.   By 1931 John Dart was again concentrating on excursions and private hire work with the "Dart Coach" and had abandoned the market bus journeys to and from Newton.   In 1932 he withdrew from the coach trade altogether, continuing as a motor and wireless engineer and he subsequently kept the Carpenters Arms in Ilsington.

There was another alternative to the "Tor Bus" for visitors wishing to reach the moors.   They could travel by rail on the Newton Abbot – Moretonhampstead branch line to Bovey Tracey, then transfer to the Great Western Railway Road Motor Services.   These ran to Haytor and Widecombe, and to Becky Falls and Manaton.   The former was competition for John Potter and Sons.

Over the next few years the "Tor Bus" service developed, with Widecombe being served every day during the summer of 1929.   Later that year it also had the benefit of a winter service for the first time.   On Wednesdays a bus left the village at 9 a.m. and 1.15 p.m., returning from Newton Abbot at 12 noon and 4.45 p.m.   There was also Bill Miner's carriers van running from Dunstone and Widecombe into Newton.

Special events brought extra traffic.   For a performance of "Midsummer Nights Dream" at Liverton in June, 1928, a special bus left Newton Abbot at 6.30 p.m., returning after the performance.   Haytor Point-to-Point Races was another popular occasion.   Buses shuttled back and forth between Newton Abbot and the course.   It was on such an occasion that an unusual passenger was carried, as this story in the local press reveals:-

"Puss in Bus.
Travels in Comfort to Point-to-Point Races: A Late Return

A cat which has lived all its life in a house adjoining Newton Abbot Market Square evidently thought that something very interesting was happening on Saturday, when large crowds assembled to catch buses for the Point-to-Point races at Haytor.

When a crowded bus was about to leave at one o'clock it was discovered that there was a stowaway on board in the shape of a cat and in consequence of the packed state of the gangway orders were given for the emergency door to be opened at the back and the cat released at that end. The passengers were under the impression that the cat had left for home, but when the bus was well on the way to Haytor the animal was found comfortably tucked up under a seat. Arriving at Haytor, it slipped out of the bus and was soon lost in the crowd which numbered several thousands.

Following the last race, scores of passenger buses and hundreds of private cars left the vicinity of Haytor and the bus in which the cat had travelled had returned to Newton Abbot on two occasions. A number of passengers who came out on the one o'clock bus returned by the last bus, which left Haytor about seven hours later, and to their astonishment in walked the cat and it duly made the return journey to Newton Abbot. On arriving in the Market Square, it jumped from the vehicle and proceeded to its home, evidently hoping that a supply of milk was ready for lapping."

Earlier, in 1930, livestock had also featured in another report:-

"Liverton : A Record?

Not only in sport does our hamlet excel, but news comes to hand that a hen belonging to Mr. J. Potter of the well-known Tor Bus Co. has successfully hatched out eighteen sturdy chicks which are now a week old and thriving well. Is this a record?"

With the introduction of the road service licensing under the 1930 Road Traffic Act, John, Sidney and Wilfred Potter, trading as J. Potter & Sons, were authorized to continue the "Tor Bus" service between Widecombe, Haytor, Ilsington, Liverton, Heathfield, Teigngrace and Newton Abbot. The fleet now consisted of three Dodge buses, two hire cars and two lorries. Premises were at Tor Garage, Haytor, the centre of operations, and at Liverton.

Life continued in the established pattern until, on 1st July, 1933, a further vehicle entered service. This was a Commer with an all-weather twenty-seat coach body, painted light green and known as the "Tor Coach. Unfortunately it had a short life in the fleet, being involved in an accident when its brakes failed on the steep Northway Hill, leading down from the moors into Widecombe. It hit a granite boulder, suffered extensive body damage and the chassis was knocked out of alignment. The vehicle was withdrawn but after repair it saw service with two other operators in Devon.

Until this time special trips were run to events such as the Air Pageant at Haldon Aerodrome or the circus performance at Torquay. Under the new regulations it was necessary to apply for authorisation for each trip, so to simplify matters a licence was obtained to operate up to two vehicles on a programme of excursions and tours from Haytor, Ilsington and Liverton. This covered race meetings, agricultural shows, fairs, fetes, dances and football. In addition there were some drives around the moor and trips to Plymouth and Torquay.

On the Widecombe – Newton Abbot bus service a special Sunday run was started. This was a "Church Bus" which left Haytor at 10.35 a.m., to arrive at Widecombe Church for eleven o'clock, returning at the conclusion of Divine Service. Wilfred Potter drove the bus which was run at the behest of Dame Violet Wills, a member of a well-known family with considerable interests in the tobacco industry. The Vicar of Ilsington at that time was thought to be High Church, whereas Dame Violet favoured a Low Church service. She therefore "encouraged" the parishioners, many of whom were her tenants, to go to Widecombe on Sundays. Wilfred Potter also regularly acted as chauffeur to Dame Violet. Dressed in uniform, leggings and cap he drove her to the family homes at Bristol and Clevedon or to see her sister in Torquay.

In March, 1934 a new make entered the fleet when a Leyland Cub was purchased. This had an extremely luxurious half-cab body by Duple which was far more comfortable than the usual service bus of the time. The interior had sun, moon and star motifs on roof of the saloon. The Leyland engine coped well with the steep hills on the "Tor Bus" route and this vehicle was the pride of the fleet.

**The early vehicles carried side route boards showing the places served.
Some of these have survived for over sixty years.**

A line up of the fleet taken in about 1927. On the right are the two Dodge buses, the first of which was christened "the pigeon basket" by visiting Staffordshire pottery workers.

A scene in Liverton village showing DV 5596 outside the shop kept by the Potter family. The hand operated petrol pump used to fill the vehicles can be seen and the building in the right background had its roof raised and floor lowered to garage the first purpose-built bus. The two people are Wilf Potter and (?)Jack Guest.

This 1929 Dodge (DV 244) was the first twenty seater in the "Tor Bus" fleet.

Forward control Leyland Cub OD 8628 was the pride of the fleet. It had a Duple body with a high standard of finish, including a pattern of sun, moon and stars on the interior roof.

BOD 841, a Dennis Ace, awaits departure in Newton Abbot Market Place in August, 1947. On the right can be seen Gourd's bus on the Bishopsteignton service. (Alan B. Cross)

A scene at the Rock Hotel, Haytor Vale, as Dennis Ace BOD 841 picks up passengers on a Newton Abbot service journey.

A Dennis Pike with a COD registration stands in Newton Abbot on 4th August, 1952. (Alan B. Cross)

The first post-war vehicle to be purchased was Bedford 29-seater HFJ 575, which is pictured here on the Newton Abbot–Haytor–Widecombe service. (R.C. Sambourne)

J. Potter & Sons provided transport for the staff of Hawkmoor Sanatorium, just off the Bovey Tracey–Moretonhampstead road.   On 4th August, 1952, KTT 492 stands in Newton Abbot waiting to work a contract journey to Hawkmoor.   (Alan B. Cross)

The chassis of this Leyland Comet is reported to have been stored in the Tor Garage for a year before being sent to Torquay for bodying by Devon Coach Builders.   The resulting complete vehicle (LDV 787) is seen in this view.

TOR BUS SERVICE.

NEWTON—HAYTOR—WIDECOMBE.
Winter Time Table

	MON., TUES., THURS., FRI.				WED. and SATS.						
LEAVE	a.m.	p.m.	p.m.	p.m.	a.m.	a.m.	p.m.	p.m.	p.m.	p.m.	
Haytor	9.35	1.35	5. 5	*8. 5	9.35	11.10	1.35	3.50	6 20	8. 5	
Ilsington	9.48	1.48	5.18	*8.18	9.48	11.23	1.48	4. 3	6.38	8.18	
Liverton	10. 0	2. 0	5.30	*8.30	10. 0	11.30	2. 0	4.15	6.45	8.30	
Heathfield	10. 5	2. 5	5.35	*8.35	10. 5	11.35	2. 5	4.20	6.50	8.35	
Teigngrace	10.10	2.10	5.40	*8.40	10.10	11.40	2.10	4.25	6.55	8.40	
Newton arr.	10.25	2.25	5.55	*8.55	10.25	11.55	2.25	4.40	7.10	8.55	

										S.	
LEAVE.											
Newton	11.45	3. 0	6.15	*9.10	10.30	12. 0	2.30	4.50	7.20	9.10	10.40
Teigngrace	11.50	3.10	6.25	*9 20	10.40	12.10	2.40	5. 0	7.30	9.20	10.50
Heathfield	12. 0	3.15	6.30	*9.25	10.45	12.15	2.45	5. 5	7.35	9.25	10.55
Liverton	12.10	3.25	6.40	*9.35	10.55	12.25	2.55	5.15	7.45	9.35	11. 5
Ilsington	12.20	3.35	6.50	*9.45	11. 5	12.35	3. 5	5.25	7.55	9.45	11.15
Haytor	12.35	3.50	7. 5	*10.0	11.10	12.50	3.20	5.40	8. 5	10. 0	11.25

S. Sats. only.

* Fridays only.

The Management cannot accept any responsibility for loss or delay on journey.

Parcels at Owner's risk.

	SUNDAYS.					SUNDAYS.				
LEAVE	a.m.	p.m.	p.m.	p.m.	p.m.		a.m.	p.m.	p.m.	p.m.	p.m.
Haytor	10.40	2. 5	5.20	8. 5	9. 5	Newton	11.30	3. 5	6 20	9.10	10. 0
Ilsington	10.53	2.18	5.33	8.18	9.18	Teigngrace	11.40	3.15	6.30	9.20	10.10
Liverton	11. 5	2.30	5.45	8.30	9.30	Heathfield	11.45	3.20	6.35	9.25	10.15
Heathfield	11.10	2.35	5.50	8.35	9.35	Liverton	11.55	3.30	6.45	9.35	10.25
Teigngrace	11.15	2.40	5.55	8.40	9.40	Ilsington	12. 5	3.40	6.55	9.45	
Newton	11.30	2.55	6.10	8.55	9.55	Haytor	12.20	3.55	7.10	10. 0	

FIRST-CLASS OPEN

AND

CLOSED CARS

FOR HIRE.

SERVICE TO WIDECOMBE WEDNESDAYS ONLY.
Leave Widecombe   9.10   1.15   6.0   Leave Newton   12 noon   4.0 p.m.

'Phone : Haytor 33.   Wire : "TORBUS, HAYTOR."
Bickington 9.

J. POTTER & SONS
TOR GARAGE, HAY TOR.

TOR BUS SERVICE.
NEWTON—HAYTOR—WIDECOMBE.

1931.   ## SUMMER SERVICES   **1931.**

(JUNE 15th to SEPTEMBER 27th.)

DEPART.	WEEK DAYS.							SUNDAYS.					
	a.m.	a.m.	p.m.	p.m.	p.m.	p.m.	p.m.	a.m.	p.m.	p.m.	p.m.	p.m.	p.m.
Widecombe	—	10.40	1.15	—	5. 0	—	7.45	—	1. 0	—	5. 0	7.45	—
Haytor	9.20	11. 0	1.35	3.30	5.20	6.20	8. 5	10.40	1.20	2.15	5.20	8. 5	9. 5
Ilsington	9.33	11.13	1.48	3.43	5.33	6.33	8.18	10.53	1.33	2.28	5.33	8.18	9.18
Liverton	9.45	11.25	2. 0	3.55	5.45	6.45	8.30	11. 5	1.45	2.40	5.45	8.30	9.30
Heathfield Cross	9.50	11.30	2. 5	4. 0	5.50	6.50	8.35	11.10	1.50	2.45	5.50	8.35	9.35
Teigngrace	9.55	11.35	2.10	4. 5	5.55	6.55	8.40	11.15	1.55	2.50	5.55	8.40	9.40
Newton Abbot arr.	10.10	11.50	2.25	4.20	6.10	7.10	8.55	11.30	2.10	3. 0	6.10	8.55	9.55

DEPART.							S.							
	a.m.	a.m.	p.m.	p.m.	p.m.	p.m.	p.m.	p.m.	p.m.	a.m.	p.m.	p.m.	p.m.	p.m.	p.m.
Newton Abbot	—	10.30	12. 0	2.30	5. 0	6 20	7.20	9.10	10 40	11.30	2.15	3. 5	6.15	9.10	10. 0
Teigngrace	—	10.40	12.10	2.40	5.10	6 30	7.30	9 20	10.50	11.40	2.25	3.15	6.25	9.20	10.10
Heathfield Cross	—	10.45	12.15	2.45	5.15	6.35	7.35	9.25	10.55	11.45	2.30	3.20	6.30	9.25	10.15
Liverton	—	10.56	12.25	2.55	5.25	6 45	7.45	9.35	11. 5	11.55	2.40	3.30	6.40	9.35	10.25
Ilsington	—	11. 5	12 35	3. 5	5.35	6 55	7.55	9.45	11.15	12. 5	2.50	3.40	6.50	9.45	—
Haytor	10.20	11.15	12.50	3.20	5.50	7.10	8. 5	9.55	11.25	12.20	3. 5	3.55	7. 5	10. 0	—
Widecombe	10.40	11.35	1.10	3.40	—	7.30	—	—	—	12.40	3.25	—	7.25	—	—

Services marked S.—Saturdays only—Theatre 'Bus.

ON WEDNESDAYS MARKET 'BUS LEAVES WIDECOMBE 9 a.m.

The Management cannot accept any responsibility for loss or delay on journey.   Parcels at Owner's risk.

FIRST-CLASS OPEN AND CLOSE CARS FOR HIRE.

'Phone : Haytor 33.   Wire : "TORBUS, HAYTOR."
Bickington 9.

J. POTTER & SONS,
TOR GARAGE, HAYTOR.

Top: timetable for the winter of 1930-31. Bottom: timetable for summer service commencing 15th June 1931.

H.674.—**Bovey Tracey** (G.W.R. Station) and **Widecombe-in-the-Moor,** via Haytor. Modifications :—
(1) To revise the time schedules as follows :—
6th July to 27th September :— Weekdays.

		a.m.	a.m.	a.m.	p.m.	p.m.	p.m.	G. p.m.	G. p.m.	p.m.	p.m.
Widecombe	dep.	—	—	10.50	12.10	—	—	—	4.40	5.45	—
Haytor	,,	9.50	10.35	11.20	12.30	2.15	2.40	3.10	4.55	6.5	7.10
Bovey Tracey	arr.	10.10	10.50	11.40	12.50	2.30	3.0	3.25	5.10	6.20	7.25

		a.m.	a.m.	a.m.	p.m.	p.m.	p.m.	p.m.	G. p.m.	p.m.	p.m.	p.m.
Bovey Tracey	dep.	10.10	11.0	11.50	—	1.0	2.35	3.10	2.35	5.10	6.35	7.50
Haytor	,,	10.30	11.20	12.10	12.50	1.20	2.55	3.25	2.55	5.25	6.55	8.10
Widecombe	arr.	10.45	11.40	—	1.10	—	—	3.40	—	5.40	7.10	—

Sundays.

		a.m.	p.m.	p.m.	p.m.	p.m.	p.m.
Widecombe	dep.	—	1.20	—	—	5.0	6.20
Haytor	,,	10.10	1.40	2.15	3.15	5.15	6.40
Ullacombe	,,	10.15	—	2.20	3.20	5.20	6.45
Bovey Tracey	arr.	10.25	—	2.30	3.30	5.35	7.0

		a.m.	p.m.	p.m.	p.m.	p.m.	p.m.	p.m.	p.m.
Bovey Tracey	dep.	11.10	—	2.35	—	3.35	5.35	7.5	8.0
Ullacombe	,,	11.15	—	2.40	—	3.40	5.40	7.10	—
Haytor	,,	11.30	12.15	2.55	3.25	3.55	5.50	7.15	8.20
Widecombe	arr.	—	12.30	—	4.0	—	6.10	—	—

G.—To operate from 3rd August to 5th September, inclusive.

Widecombe Fair :—To operate journeys to Widecombe from all trains arriving at Bovey Tracey from 10.7 a.m. up to 6.24 p.m. ; also to operate return journeys to meet traffic requirements.

28th September to 25th October, and 3rd May to 4th July :—
Weekdays only.

		a.m.	p.m.	p.m.				a.m.	p.m.	p.m.
Haytor	dep.	10.0	1.30	5.40	Bovey Tracey	dep.	11.10	2.45	6.30
Ullacombe	,,	10.5	1.35	5.45	Ullacombe	,,	11.20	2.55	6.40
Bovey Tracey	arr.	10.18	1.45	6.0	Haytor	arr.	11.30	3.5	6.50

26th October to 2nd May :—To suspend the service.

(2) To revise the fare schedule as follows :—
Bovey Tracey.
3d. — Edgehill.
6d. 9d. 3d. — Ullacombe.
9d. 1/3 6d. — 3d. — Green Lane.
1/- 1/6 9d. — 6d. 10d. 3d. — Haytor.
1/4 2/- 1/1 1/6 10d. 1/3 7d. 1/- 4d. — Hemsworthy.
1/6 2/3 1/3 2/- 1/1 1/6 9d. 1/3 6d. — 2d. — Haresfoot.
1/9 3/- 1/6 2/6 1/3 2/3 1/1 1/8 10d. 1/3 6d. 10d. 5d. — Widecombe.
S. R. S. R. S. R. S. R. S. R. S. R. S. R.
S.—Single fares. R.—Return fares.
To issue cheap day returns to and from Bovey Tracey (G.W.R. Station) and Widecombe, 2/6 ; also circular cheap day returns, 2/6 from any stage.
To charge a fare of 2d. to passengers desiring to travel a distance of one mile or less between any two stages on the route.

H.675.—**Bovey Tracey** (G.W.R. Station) and **Manaton,** via Becky Falls. Modifications :—
(1) To operate the service from 6th July to 27th September, in accordance with the following revised time schedule :— Weekdays. Sundays.

		a.m.	p.m.	p.m.	p.m.	G. p.m.	a.m.	p.m.	p.m.
Bovey Tracey	dep.	11.0	1.0	3.25	5.35	6.30	11.10	2.40	6.20
Manaton	arr.	11.20	1.20	3.45	5.55	6.50	11.30	3.0	6.40

		a.m.	a.m.	p.m.	p.m.	p.m.	G. p.m.	a.m.	p.m.	p.m.	p.m.
Manaton	dep.	10.25	11.40	2.10	4.50	6.0	6.55	10.5	2.5	5.10	6.40
Bovey Tracey	arr.	10.45	12.5	2.30	5.10	6.20	7.15	10.25	2.25	5.30	7.0

G.—To operate from 3rd August to 5th September, inclusive.

(2) To suspend the service from 28th September to 5th July.

(3) To charge a fare of 2d. to passengers desiring to travel a distance of one mile or less between any two stages on the route.

18

H.1421.—**Newton Abbot** and **Dunstone,** via Teigngrace, Heathfield Cross, Liverton, Ilsington, Haytor and Widecombe-in-the-Moor. Modifications :—

(1) To revise the time schedules as follows :—
6th July to 27th September, inclusive :—

					W.O.				Weekdays.					C.		Sundays.				
					a.m.	a.m.	p.m.	p.m.	p.m.	p.m.	p.m.	p.m.	a.m.	p.m.	p.m.	p.m.	p.m.	p.m.	p.m.
Dunstone	..	..	..	dep.	9.5	—	—	—	—	—	—	—	—	—	—	—	—	—	—
Widecombe	..	..	..	,,	9.10	—	10.50	1.20	—	4.40	5.45	7.30	—	12.10	1.20	—	5.0	7.30	—
Haytor	..	..	..	,,	9.30	9.30	11.10	1.40	4.0	5.5	6.5	7.45	10.40	12.30	1.40	2.30	5.25	7.45	8.45
Liverton	..	..	..	,,	—	9.53	11.33	2.3	4.23	5.28	6.28	8.8	11.3	—	2.0	2.50	5.48	8.8	9.5
Heathfield	..	..	..	,,	—	10.0	11.40	2.10	4.30	5.35	6.35	8.15	11.10	—	2.8	2.58	5.55	8.15	9.13
Teigngrace	..	..	..	,,	—	10.5	11.45	2.15	4.35	5.40	6.40	8.20	11.15	—	2.13	3.3	6.0	8.20	9.18
Newton Abbot	..	..	..	arr.	—	10.25	11.55	2.25	4.50	5.55	6.55	8.35	11.28	—	2.25	3.15	6.10	8.35	9.30

			W.O.							W.S.	W.O.	S.							
			a.m.	p.m.		p.m.	p.m.	p.m.	p.m.	p.m.	p.m.		a.m.	a.m.	p.m.	p.m.	p.m.	p.m.	p.m.
Newton Abbot	dep.		10.35	12.0	2.35	4.0	5.0	6.15	7.0	9.15	10.15	—	11.15	—	11.30	2.35	3.30	6.15	9.15	10.0
Teigngrace	,,		10.45	12.10	2.45	4.10	5.10	6.25	7.10	9.25	10.25	—	11.25	—	11.40	2.45	3.40	6.25	9.25	10.10
Heathfield	,,		10.50	12.15	2.50	4.15	5.15	6.30	7.15	9.30	10.30	—	11.30	—	11.45	2.50	3.45	6.30	9.30	10.15
Liverton	,,		11.0	12.25	3.0	4.25	5.25	6.40	7.25	9.40	10.40	10.40	11.40	—	11.55	3.0	3.55	6.40	9.40	10.25
Haytor	,,		11.20	12.50	3.25	4.50	5.45	6.55	7.45	10.0	—	11.0	11.55	10.35	12.15	3.25	4.15	6.55	10.0	10.45
Widecombe	,,		11.40	1.10	3.40	5.10	—	7.15	—	—	—	—	—	10.55	12.35	3.40	—	7.15	—	—
Dunstone	arr.		—	—	5.15	—	—	—	—	—	—	—	—	—	—	—	—	—	—	—

W.O.—Wednesdays only. S.—Saturdays only. W.S.—Wednesdays and Saturdays only. C.—Awaits conclusion of Church Service.

28th September to 5th July :—

Mondays, Tuesdays, Thursdays and Fridays.

				P.	P.	F.			C.	Sundays.				
				a.m.	a.m.	p.m.	p.m.	p.m.	a.m.	p.m.	p.m.	p.m.	p.m.	p.m.
Widecombe	..	..	dep.	—	—	—	—	—	—	12.10	—	—	—	—
Haytor	..	..	,,	9.30	11.10	1.40	5.5	7.15	10.40	12.30	2.0	5.30	8.5	9.0
Liverton	..	..	,,	9.53	11.33	2.3	5.28	7.38	11.3	—	2.23	5.53	8.28	9.23
Heathfield	..	..	,,	10.0	11.40	2.10	5.35	7.45	11.10	—	2.30	6.0	8.35	9.30
Teigngrace	..	..	,,	10.5	11.45	2.15	5.40	7.50	11.15	—	2.35	6.5	8.40	9.35
Newton Abbot	..	..	arr.	10.20	11.55	2.25	5.55	8.5	11.28	—	2.50	6.15	8.55	9.50

				P.				F.	C.				
				a.m.	a.m.	p.m.	p.m.	p.m.	a.m.	p.m.	p.m.	p.m.	p.m.
Newton Abbot	..	..	dep.	10.30	12.0	3.0	6.20	9.15	—	11.30	3.0	6.20	9.15
Teigngrace	..	..	,,	10.40	12.10	3.10	6.30	9.25	—	11.40	3.10	6.30	9.25
Heathfield	..	..	,,	10.45	12.15	3.15	6.35	9.30	—	11.45	3.15	6.35	9.30
Liverton	..	..	,,	10.55	12.25	3.25	6.45	9.40	—	11.55	3.25	6.45	9.40
Haytor	..	..	,,	11.10	12.50	3.50	7.5	10.0	10.35	12.10	3.45	7.5	10.0
Widecombe	..	..	arr.	—	—	—	—	—	10.55	—	—	—	—

P.—From 28th September to 25th October and 3rd May to 4th July. F.—Fridays only from 26th October to 2nd May. C.—Awaits conclusion of Church Service.

Wednesdays and Saturdays.

				W.O.			W.O.			W.O.	S.O.			
				a.m.	a.m.	a.m.	p.m.	p.m.	p.m.	p.m.	p.m.	p.m.	p.m.	p.m.
Dunstone	..	..	dep.	9.5	—	—	—	—	—	5.10	—	—	—	—
Widecombe	..	..	,,	9.10	—	—	1.20	—	—	5.15	—	—	—	—
Haytor	..	..	,,	9.30	9.30	11.10	1.40	1.40	4.0	5.30	—	6.30	8.10	—
Liverton	..	..	,,	—	9.53	11.33	—	2.3	4.23	—	5.30	6.50	8.30	9.45	10.45
Heathfield	..	..	,,	—	10.0	11.40	—	2.10	4.30	—	5.38	6.58	8.38	9.53	10C50
Teigngrace	..	..	,,	—	10.5	11.45	—	2.15	4.35	—	5.43	7.3	8.43	9.38	10.55
Newton Abbot	..	..	arr.	—	10.20	11.55	—	2.25	4.50	—	5.55	7.15	9.0	10.10	11.5

			W.O.				W.O.	S.O.		S.O.					W.O.	S.O.
			a.m.	p.m.	p.m.	p.m.	p.m.	p.m.	p.m.	p.m.	p.m.	p.m.	p.m.	p.m.	p.m.	p.m.
Newton Abbot	..	dep.	10.30	12.0	—	3.0	4.0	5.0	5.45	6.15	7.20	9.15	10.15	—	11.15
Teigngrace	..	,,	10.40	12.10	—	3.10	4.10	5.10	5.55	6.25	7.30	9.25	10.25	—	11.25
Heathfield	..	,,	10.45	12.15	—	3.15	4.15	5.15	6.0	6.30	7.35	9.30	10.30	—	11.30
Liverton	..	,,	10.55	12.25	—.	3.25	4.25	5.25	6.10	6.40	7.45	9.40	10.40	10.40	11.40
Haytor	..	,,	11.10	12.45	12.45	3.45	4.45	—	—	6.30	—	8.5	10.0	—	11.0	12.0
Widecombe	..	,,	—	—	1.5	—	5.5	—	—	—	—	—	—	—	—
Dunstone	..	arr.	—	—	—	—	5.10	—	—	—	—	—	—	—	—

S.O.—Saturdays only. W.O.—Wednesdays only. C.—10.50 ex Heathfield calls main Cross Roads only.

(2) To introduce a day return and circular fare of 4/6 between Newton Abbot and Haytor.

(3) To charge a fare of 2d. to passengers desiring to travel a distance of one mile or less between any two stages on the route.

Above and opposite: applications for revised timetables published in Notices & Proceedings on 17th August 1936.

Chapter Three : J. Potter & Sons Limited

On the merging of the operations of the Great Western Railway Road Motor Services with the motor bus services of the National Omnibus & Transport Co. Ltd in 1929, a new company, Western National Omnibus Co. Ltd was formed. This took over operation of the two railway bus services from Bovey Tracey Station – to Becky Falls and Manaton, and to Haytor and Widecombe.

However, both these routes and that between Chagford and Moretonhampstead Station were detached from the main Western National operating area. All were partially dependent upon summer tourists and on the two Bovey Tracey routes in particular winter traffic was very thin. The buses were kept in a garage at the Dolphin Hotel but with the costs of a distant out-station, difficult routes and highly seasonal traffic, they were not particularly remunerative.

The Chagford–Moretonhampstead service shared a common route with a service operated by Devon General, in which the railway now also had an interest. Therefore, arrangements were made to transfer these Western National operations to the Devon General company. The latter, however, had no desire to take on the marginal Bovey Tracey services, so J. Potter & Sons were approached with a view to their taking them over. The Bovey Tracey–Haytor–Widecombe service competed for traffic with the "Tor Bus" Newton Abbot–Haytor–Widecombe route and so it was agreed that Potter & Sons would assume responsibilty for both Bovey - Widecombe (Western National Service 122) and Bovey - Manaton (Western National Service 123). "Tor Bus" were due to start on 1st January, 1935 but, in fact, the actual date of commencement was Wednesday 23rd January.

During the winter months both services ran on Wednesdays and Saturdays only, the Widecombe route being curtailed at Haytor. During summer operation increased to daily, with through running to Widecombe. Connections were made at Bovey Tracey Station with the Great Western Railway trains on the Moretonhampstead–Newton Abbot branch line. The bus time tables were arranged so that all journeys on both routes could be covered by one vehicle, usually one of the two surviving Dodges.

In February, 1935, John Potter retired at the age of seventy-three and the ownership of the business passed to his sons, Sidney and Wilfred. They continued to trade as J. Potter & Sons, with the fleet name "Tor Bus".

The following month saw mid-Devon experience its heaviest fall of snow for the winter, with drifts several feet deep. Bus services were affected and some Devon General services were cancelled. The "Tor Bus" battled on but had to suspend that part of the route between Liverton and Haytor, always a challenge in snow and icy conditions.

1935 was the Silver Jubilee of the accession to the throne of King George V and Queen Mary. Throughout the country there was rejoicing. In Ilsington the Church Bells ushered in the day of celebration and the village and schools were tastefully decorated. After a thanksgiving service and sports, there was a meat tea for all parishioners and in the evening over 2,000 people congregated on Haytor for a bonfire and community singing. Potters' buses conveyed the children and the old people to and from the village.

New and second-hand vehicles were purchased during 1935. The first was a second-hand Maudslay. This had no self-starter and so required two people on the starting handle to make it roar into life. It did have the benefit of a large engine beneath its big bonnet and would complete the climb from Liverton up to Haytor with a full load, something the early buses could not be relied upon to do. At first it was run in a blue livery, before being repainted into "Tor Bus" colours.

In March a new Dennis Ace was purchased. The snout like bonnet, which protruded beyond the front axle of this model, caused it to be known as the "Flying Pig" but its short wheelbase gave it excellent manoeuvreability. To complete the year's intake two Leyland Cubs were delivered, although these were normal-control models whereas the 1934 vehicle was forward-control, half-cab. The Cubs were popular, particularly on the notorious Northway hill near Widecombe and on the long climb from Liverton, through Ilsington to Haytor. On the latter, bottom gear was needed to ascend in a private car but each of the three "Tor Bus" Cubs could tackle it successfully in second gear.

The Widecombe–Newton Abbot route was extended in this year to serve the hamlet of Dunstone, to the south of Widecombe. This was the home of Bill Miners, haulier, bus operator and colourful local character. The "Tor Bus" left Dunstone at 9.10 a.m. each Wednesday for Newton, running just behind Miner's service from Challacombe to Newton Abbot which had been introduced in 1934. There was also some housing development at Heathfield, near Candy's Works. Non-parlour, three-bedroom houses on the Heather Estate, with all the latest conveniences and good gardens, were available for £10 down and buy at ten shillings and sixpence a week. The inhabitants provided some extra traffic for the buses.

On 2nd September, 1935, the two Potter brothers formed a limited liability company, J. Potter & Sons Ltd. This took over the business of garage and omnibus proprietors, including three bus services, excursions and tours, private party coach hire, taxis and lorries. The rolling stock consisted of seven public service vehicles – 2 Dodge buses (20 seaters), 3 Leyland Cubs (26 seaters), 1 Maudslay (25 seater) and a Dennis Ace (20 seater); there were also a six-seater landaulette, a four/five seater car and 2 Dodge two-ton lorries. The directors were Sidney and Wilfred Potter and the nominal capital was £2,500 in £1 shares.

Attention was now given to making the moorland routes more remunerative. It was perceived that if better connections could be offered between the three services, and if they could be linked across previously unserved moorland roads, the potential for tourist traffic would be increased. It was also hoped to serve additional settlements on the market services.

The first plan was to re-route the Dunstone market buses to run through Widecombe, Manaton and Bovey Tracey. This was opposed by Mr A.E. Thomas of Chagford, who already operated a market day bus through Manaton to and from Newton Abbot. There was also opposition from Devon General, who were no doubt fearful of possible "Tor Bus" ambitions on the Bovey Tracey–Newton Abbot section which the company covered frequently. The objections were upheld and Dunstone continued to be served by an extension of the Newton Abbot–Haytor–Widecombe service.

Undaunted by this rebuff, J. Potter & Sons again proposed to run between Dunstone, Widecombe, Manaton and Newton Abbot, some journeys routed via Heytree Cross, Manaton and Becky Falls; others over a section of route commanding beautiful views. The route crossed Trendlebere Down by a road known as Terrace Drive, joining the main Widecombe–Newton Abbot route at Haytor. Circular trip tickets were envisaged. This proposal, too, was opposed by A.E. Thomas and also by the Newton Abbot Rural District Council. The authority were concerned about buses using Terrace Drive, even though it was proposed to use nothing bigger than a 14-seater (which size the company did not then own). In the face of these objections the applications were withdrawn and the Potter brothers decided to make the best of a bad job and keep to the existing routes, but to withdraw the two Bovey Tracey services between the end of October and the beginning of May each year.

The 1936 addition to the fleet was a second Dennis Ace delivered in August. Also, at about this time, the oldest of the two surviving Dodge buses was converted to a lorry. During the year the family were saddened by the death, on 22nd July, of Mr. John Potter at the age of seventy-four.

The years 1936 and 1937 brought changes in timings on all services and the discontinuance of the route extension to Dunstone, traffic from this small settlement being left to Bill Miners. The bus fleet was reduced from its peak of seven to five, the Maudslay and the first of the Dennis Aces being withdrawn.

With war imminent, services were again revised in 1939, both times and periods of operation being amended. Also, for the first time, some journeys on the Newton Abbot–Widecombe service ran direct between Newton and Exeter Cross, omitting Teigngrace and Heathfield. The last Dodge bus was withdrawn and its replacement was a rare vehicle, a Dennis Pike (with a COD registration), delivered in August, 1939.

Therefore, at the declaration of war on 3rd September, 1939, there were three Leyland and two Dennis buses, two Austin taxis and a 5-6 ton lorry used for stone haulage. The first casualty of war was the 1939 Widecombe

Fair. Instead of being thick with crowds of people, rows of motor cars and coaches, stalls, pony and sheep pens, Widecombe slept peacefully in the moor on the second Tuesday in September. It was a great blow to the villagers as the weather was perfect, and also resulted in the loss to J. Potter & Sons Ltd of the major revenue earning day of the year.

From Monday, 16th October a national emergency service timetable was introduced on the Newton Abbot–Widecombe route. Both the Bovey Tracey services were suspended, never to return, and the excursions and tours ceased for the duration of hostilities.

Wartime conditions resulted in many difficulties. There was a shortage of spare parts and tyres; fuel supplies were strictly rationed. To avoid vehicles being seen at night by enemy aircraft, headlights and interior lights were masked. To drive a bus along narrow, twisting Devon lanes with only a pencil of light for visibility was quite an experience. Mudguards were lined in white to enable vehicles to be better seen in the dark by pedestrians. The lack of petrol for private cars forced those who had previously driven themselves to ride on the buses. In addition, the dangers of bombing in the cities meant that many urban dwellers moved into the relative safety of the countryside. The consequence was an upsurge in the number of passengers carried.

Particularly affected by the evacuation from the cities were children. They had to leave homes and parents to be taken by train to distant destinations where they were billeted with temporary parents. For many children this was the first time they had been separated from their family and, for some, the very first experience of life in the country. Some adjusted easily but for others it was a terrifying, traumatic experience. Many children from London came to the Ilsington and Liverton area and stayed with local people.

From the summer of 1940 Devon County Council hired a "Tor Bus" each day to take these evacuees from Ilsington and Liverton to school at Blackpool, a 20 or 26-seater being used, for which the payment to J. Potter & Sons was £1 per day. In the autumn these journeys were extended through to Newton Abbot, where some of the children now attended school.

As the bombing of London intensified there were fears for the safety of the evacuee children's parents. Mr. Sidney Potter visited the capital and found that many of the fathers worked in the docks on essential war work and could not leave. However, he arranged for a lot of the mothers to be moved down to Haytor and two twenty-seater buses were despatched to the East End of London. They arrived back, fully loaded, at ten o'clock at night and then somewhere had to be arranged for the women to stay. Bert Frost, senior driver for the firm for many years, recollected that Mr Philp at Honeywill Farm took seven. Some of the people eventually settled in the area and their children grew up, married and had children of their own.

Although large numbers of passengers presented themselves for many journeys, the rationing of fuel meant that it was not possible to run a duplicate

TOR BUS SERVICE

NEWTON (Market Square)—HAYTOR—WIDECOMBE (WEEKDAYS)
National Emergency Service from Monday, October 16th, until further notice

Depart	Mon. Tues. Thur. Fri. a.m.	p.m.	p.m.	Wednesdays and Saturdays a.m. W.	a.m.	a.m.	p.m.	p.m.	p.m. W.	p.m.	p.m.
Widecombe				9.15					4.45		
Haytor M.H.	9.30	1.40	4.45	9.30	9.30	11.10	1.40	3.30	5. 0	5.15	8. 0
Ilsington	9.40	1.50	4.55		9.40	11.20	1.50	3.40		5.25	8.10
Liverton	9.50	2. 0	5. 5		9.50	11.30	2. 0	3.50		5.35	8.20
Heathfield	10. 0	2.10	5.15		10. 0	11.40	2.10	4. 0		5.45	8.30
Teigngrace	10.5	2.15	5.20		10. 5	11.45	2.15	4. 5		5.50	8.35
Newton A. (arr.)	10.20	2.30	5.35		10.20	11.58	2.30	4.20		6. 5	8.50

Depart	Mon. Tues. Thur. Fri. a.m.	p.m.	p.m.	Wednesdays and Saturdays a.m. W.	a.m.	p.m.	p.m.	p.m.	p.m. S.O.	p.m.	p.m.
Newton Abbot	12. 0	3.30	6. 0	10.30	12. 0	2.35	3.30	4.30	6.15	7. 0	9.15
Teigngrace	12.10	3.40	6.10	10.40	12.10	2.45	3.40	4.40	6.25	7.10	9.25
Heathfield	12.15	3.45	6.15	10.45	12.15	2.50	3.45	4.45	6.30	7.15	9.30
Liverton	12.25	3.55	6.25	10.55	12.25	3. 0	3.55	4.55	6.40	7.25	9.40
Ilsington	12.35	4. 5	6.35	11. 3	12.35	3.10	4. 5	5. 5		7.35	9.50
Haytor M.H.	12.50	4.15	6.45	11.10	12.50	3.25	4.15	5.15		7.50	10.0
Widecombe (arr.)							4.35				

W.   Wednesdays only

NEWTON (Market Square)—HAYTOR—WIDECOMBE.   SUNDAYS.

Depart	a.m.	p.m. C.	p.m.	p.m.	p.m.
Widecombe		12.10			
Haytor (Moorland Hotel)	10.40	12.30	2. 0	5.30	8. 0
Ilsington	10.50		2.10	5.40	8.10
Liverton	11. 0		2.20	5.50	8.20
Heathfield	11.10		2.30	6. 0	8.30
Teigngrace	11.15		2.35	6. 5	8.35
Newton Abbot (arr.)	11.28		2.50	6.15	8.50

Depart	a.m.	a.m.	p.m.	p.m.	p.m.
Newton Abbot		11.30	3. 0	6.20	9.15
Teigngrace		11.40	3.10	6.30	9.25
Heathfield		11.45	3.15	6.35	9.30
Liverton		11.55	3.25	6.45	9.40
Ilsington	C.	12. 5	3.35	6.55	9.50
Haytor (Moorland Hotel)	10.35	12.15	3.45	7. 5	10.0
Widecombe (arr.)	10.55				

C.   Church Bus awaits conclusion of service.

Cut out and keep by you.   **J. POTTER AND SONS, HAYTOR.**

Emergency service timetable introduced after the outbreak of war in 1939.

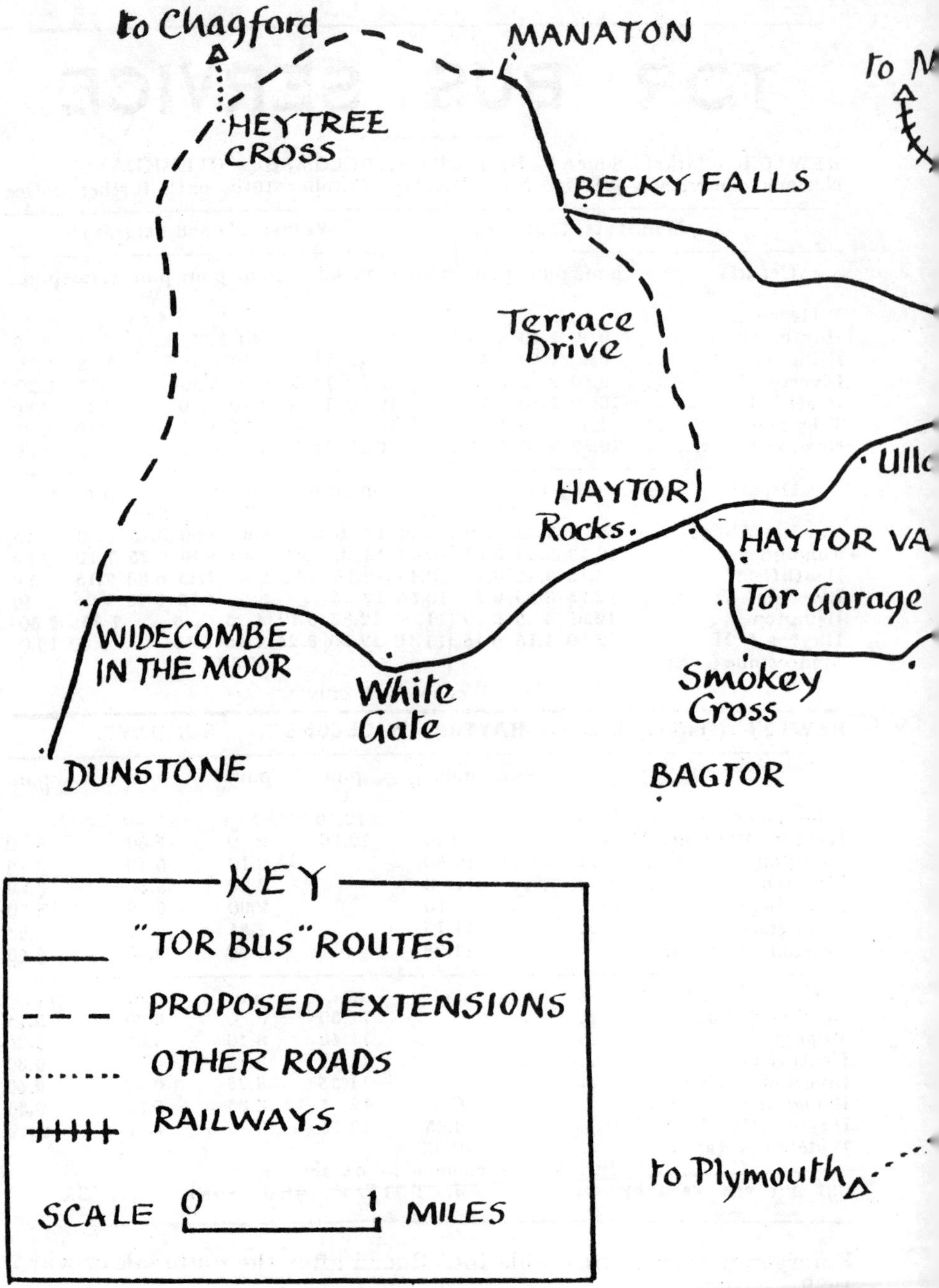

to Chagford

MANATON

to M

HEYTREE
CROSS

BECKY FALLS

Terrace
Drive

HAYTOR
Rocks.

Ullo

HAYTOR VA

Tor Garage

WIDECOMBE
IN THE MOOR

White
Gate

Smokey
Cross

DUNSTONE

BAGTOR

—KEY—

_____ "TOR BUS" ROUTES

_ _ _ PROPOSED EXTENSIONS

.... OTHER ROADS

+++++ RAILWAYS

SCALE 0 _____ 1 MILES

to Plymouth

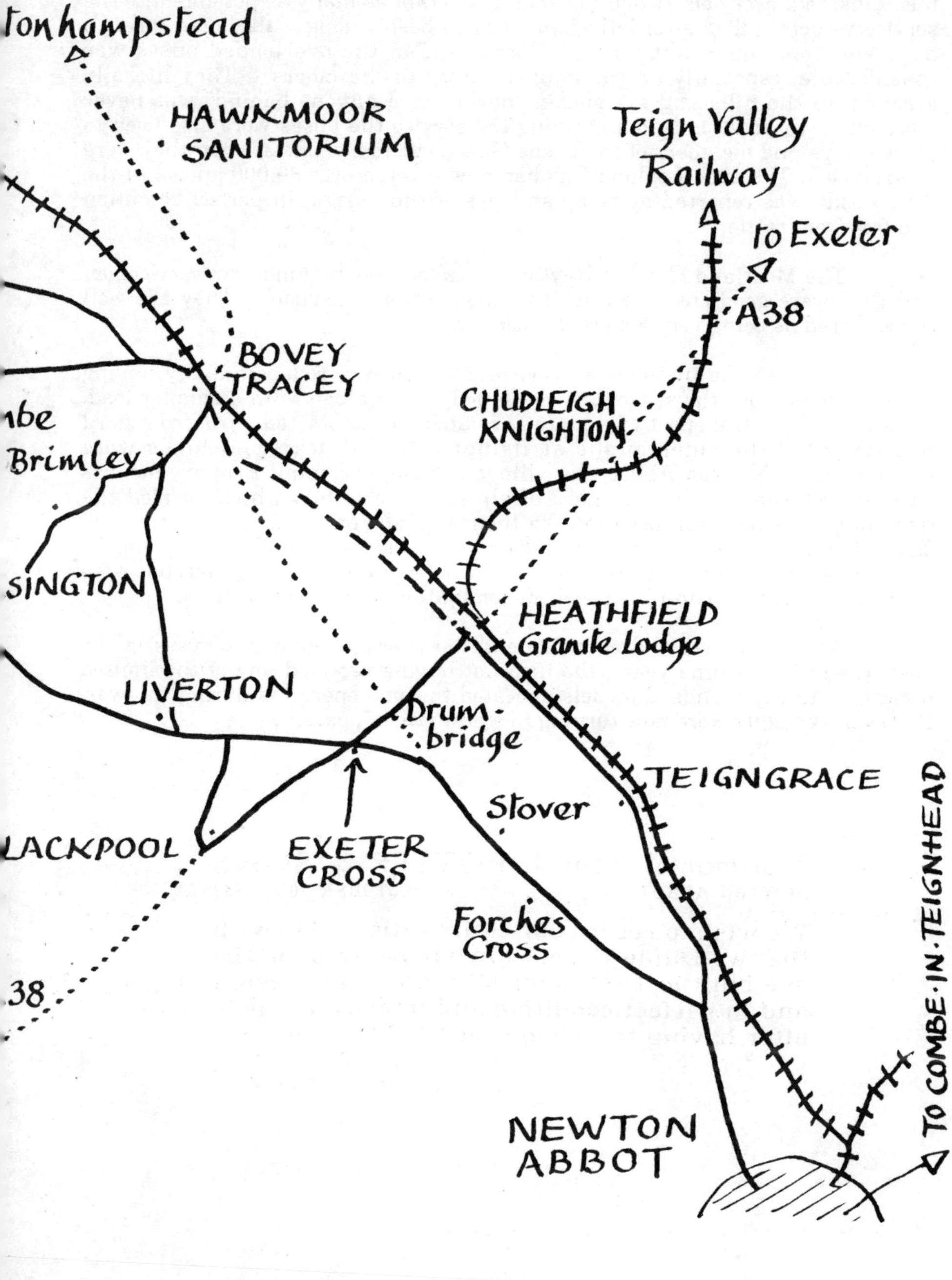

ton hampstead

HAWKMOOR
SANITORIUM

Teign Valley
Railway

to Exeter

A38

BOVEY
TRACEY

CHUDLEIGH
KNIGHTON

mbe
Brimley

HEATHFIELD
Granite Lodge

SINGTON

LIVERTON

Drum-
bridge

TEIGNGRACE

Stover

LACKPOOL

EXETER
CROSS

Forches
Cross

38

NEWTON
ABBOT

TO COMBE·IN·TEIGNHEAD

bus. Instead, every effort had to be made to cram as many as possible into the service vehicle. The alternative would have been a long walk home through dark and sometimes wet lanes. The strain on the overloaded buses was considerable, especially on the long climb up to the moors. They literally groaned up the hills and the slogan "never leave anyone behind" was never more apt. In addition to maintaining the service the buses were also used to carry troops and members of the Home Guard out to Dartmoor when they were on exercise. The 1934 Leyland Cub had now covered over 80,000 miles but the Duple body was reported as being still modern in design, in perfect condition and free from rattle.

The Moorland Hotel at Haytor was taken over by American servicemen and they were good customers for the taxis run by the firm. They are well remembered as being very generous with tips.

By 1943 the number of evacuee children had reduced, many having returned home, but the school bus continued to run albeit with a smaller load. However, school transport of a more permanent kind started. As from 23rd August, 1943 the older pupils at Ilsington and Blackpool schools were transferred to Newton Abbot, the village schools becoming Primary schools only, rather than taking scholars of all ages. The bus which carried the remaining evacuees was used to take them to and from their new school each day. Requests that children attending private schools in Newton Abbot be allowed to ride were refused but Roman Catholic pupils living at Liverton were permitted to travel to and from their denominational school in Newton.

As the war years drew to an end the average age of the buses in the fleet was just over nine years, the firm not having received any of the limited number of utility standard models allocated to some operators during the war. However, thoughts were now turning to a new era, of peace.

Testimonial from **J. POTTER & SONS**
NEWTON ABBOT   **OCTOBER 20th, 1941**

We wish to record our entire satisfaction with the two Duple Coaches in our possession, the one built in 1934 being still modern in design and in perfect condition and free from rattle after having travelled over 80,000 miles.

Original can be seen with others at Duple Works

Chapter Four : Post War Peak

Although the war ended in 1945 vehicles remained in short supply and it was not possible either to replace the ageing fleet or to expand it to meet the needs of a population which, freed from the restrictions and rigours of wartime Britain, wanted to travel.

There were villagers, travelling in and out of Newton Abbot for shopping, the market or the cinema; in summer visitors going out to the moors and to Widecombe. Duplicate buses were frequently needed and Saturday evenings were particularly busy, it not being unusual for two duplicates to be needed on the last bus out of Newton Abbot when people came home from the pub and cinema. Summer Sundays were also busy with many visitors having a day out on the moors.

The excursions operated in pre-war days were resumed and private hire work increased as pub, club, church, chapel and Womens Institute members went on outings or cricket and football club teams and their supporters were transported to away matches. A new pastime, cycle speedway, also resulted in private hire work for the "Tor Bus", with supporters of the Bickington team following their local boys.

The winter of 1946-47 brought dreadful weather conditions with the West Country buried under the heaviest fall of snow for fifty years. The moorland roads were covered by enormous drifts and the "Tor Bus" could not reach Widecombe for several weeks.

By 1947 the average age of the bus fleet was eleven years and so, when the first new post-war vehicle arrived in August of that year, it was very welcome. HFJ 575 was a Bedford OB model with a 29-seat coach body, the interior decor of which closely resembled that used by Greenslades Tours of Exeter. It has been suggested that it was intended for the Exeter firm and when not required by them, was eagerly snapped up by J. Potter & Sons. It was much needed as in the spring of that year a contract had been entered into with Devon County Council Education Department to convey schoolchildren between Hennock and Newton Abbot. Payment for the 29-seater called for was £3. 12s. 0d. per day, a good price at the time.

In the previous year an application for an increase in the daily rate for the Ilsington–Newton Abbot school contract from £1. 15s. 0d. to £2. 8s. 0d. had been refused, but a compromise reached at £2. 5s. 0d. With the raising of the school leaving age as from the autumn of 1947 the numbers travelling from Ilsington and Liverton increased and a 26-seater had to be provided at an extra half-crown (2s. 6d.) a day to replace the 20-seater which had been used for some time.

On New Years Day, 1949, a second new Bedford entered service, this carrying a bus body with wooden seats for thirty-one passengers. The extra capacity was useful and its arrival allowed the withdrawal, soon after, of the 1936 Dennis Ace. The fleet then numbered six buses and coaches plus two taxis. The goods transport side of the business had ceased.

The Widecombe–Newton Abbot service pattern was similar to pre-war days, with Widecombe being served on Wednesdays and Saturdays in winter, daily in summer. A daily service was maintained between Haytor and Newton throughout the year. The Sunday morning Church bus to Widecombe had been discontinued and more journeys used the direct route via Forches Cross, serving a hostel for Polish people at Stover. This settlement could provide almost a full load of passengers to and from Newton Abbot at times and in the season many Poles would go out to Dartmoor on the "Tor Bus" to gather whortleberries.

In 1949 the bus business of Mr W. Miners of Dunstone was acquired by Wilfred Beard of Ponsworthy, with whom J. Potter & Sons enjoyed a friendly relationship. He abandoned the Challacombe–Dunstone–Widecombe–Newton Abbot market service which had competed on part of the "Tor Bus" route. Bill Miners continued as a haulage contractor for many years.

During 1950 the Potter brothers placed in service three new vehicles, all different makes. The first was a Leyland Comet, fitted with a 5-litre oil engine, five-speed gearbox and vacuum hydraulic brakes. It appears that the chassis had been stored at the Tor Garage for almost a year before being bodied by Devon Coach Builders at Torquay.

In July, an unusual vehicle, a four-cylinder Sentinel, integrally constructed, with an underfloor engine and body by Beadle, joined the fleet. It had seating for forty passengers, making it the largest vehicle operated to date and the first of its kind in the area. Above the side windows appeared the names of the main places served – Widecombe, Haytor, Newton. It had been displayed at the 1949 Commercial Motor Show and cost J. Potter & Sons £4,000. It had a David Brown gearbox and a most unusual engine note. The combination of a four-cylinder engine and the high seating capacity was a considerable challenge and engine vibration caused some difficulties in the linkage to the gearbox. On one occasion the bus was kept in service by Fred Pady, the mechanic, taking up the gangway floorboards and laying down in the aisle. Each time the driver, Bert Frost, wanted to change gear he would shout "O.K. Fred" and Fred would ensure the change, assisted by a loop of string. Subsequently a six-cylinder Sentinel was demonstrated to the firm but no vehicles of this type were purchased. For one local man the arrival of the Sentinel was a disappointment. In his eyes it did not match up to the Sentinel steam lorries from Exwick Mills, in the city of Exeter, which in the old days would pass along the turnpike road (A38) to the south of Liverton, on their way to Plymouth with loads of flour. The faint hiss of the steamer had been music to his ears. The engine note of the newcomer was certainly not musical!

To complete the year's deliveries another 29-seater Bedford coach (MTA 554) was bought in September. Maintenance of the OB model was quite the opposite of the troublesome Sentinel. Fred Pady recalls being able to reline a clutch on the Bedford in three-quarters of an hour, working on his own.

As a result of these acquisitions the last two Leyland Cubs, AUO 712 and AUO 713, were withdrawn from service. The wooden framed body on one of them was showing distinct signs of wear. A local farmer who travelled to school on it at the time remembers that daylight could be seen between the body panels. The other had apparently been partially rebuilt for it carried a plate from a firm called Vigars, who had seemingly renovated it at some time. One of them became a living van for a well known local character around Bovey Tracey, "old gypsy Small", who went by this name even when he was a young man. In their final years the Cubs were "thirsty" and frequent attention from a can of water was essential if a sudden cloud of steam from the radiator was to be avoided.

At the beginning of 1950 the County Council reviewed the school transport arrangements in the Newton Abbot area. The Hennock–Newton Abbot contract, held by J. Potter & Sons, was among those re-opened to tender. As a result of tenders received the new contract for the route was awarded to H.D. Gourd & Sons of Bishopsteignton and "Tor Bus" operation ceased. This left only one vehicle on school work. However, contract work was also undertaken for Hawkmoor Sanatorium, a chest hospital just off the Moretonhampstead road to the north of Bovey Tracey. Nursing and other staff were carried to and from Newton Abbot at the beginning and end of periods of duty. Another regular contract run which started in the 1950s was the weekly "welfare bus". This left Haytor at 2 p.m. and took mothers and children to and from the clinic at Bovey Tracey.

During 1952 most of the service journeys were diverted between Liverton and Exeter Cross to run via Blackpool School, thence along the A38. In June of that year Wilfred Potter, the youngest of the two brothers who owned the company, died at the age of 54. In the following year his brother Sidney also passed away at the age of 57. This left their widows and Wilfred's daughter, Muriel (Bunclark) to run the business. They were joined by Sid Brinicombe, John Potter's nephew. Mr H.W. Brockway, a very tall man always known as Tiny was the secretary of the company. He is remembered with affection by many in the area.

1953 brought the end of an era when the last Dennis – the Pike – was withdrawn, but also the beginning of another with the purchase of the first A.E.C. for the firm. It had long been Bert Frost's ambition to see this make in the fleet and now his wish had come true. The eight feet wide, thirty feet long vehicle had a fluid flywheel, synchromesh gearbox and air brakes. This was a big vehicle for the country lanes and moorland roads traversed by the "Tor Bus" service and it was disposed of after only two years service. At this time most of the fleet were garaged at the Tor Garage, Haytor, but two vehicles were kept overnight at a gravel dump near the Moorland Hotel, Haytor.

31

A new development on the bus service was the introduction of early morning journeys for workers. As from 1st April, 1954, a bus left Haytor at 7.3 a.m, travelling via Ilsington, Liverton, Blackpool, Heathfield and Teigngrace to arrive in Newton Abbot at 7.45am. It then returned via Teigngrace, Heathfield, Exeter Cross and Liverton to Ilsington. Initially introduced for an experimental period of three months it proved successful and survived after the end of the trial. Later a second journey was introduced, leaving Haytor at 8.10 a.m. and arriving in Newton Abbot ten minutes before nine o'clock.

During these post-war years there were constant changes in timings but the general level of service remained unchanged. However, there were signs that passenger numbers were beginning to decline as more and more people bought cars or motor cycles and stopped using the buses.

TOR BUS SERVICE

MARCH 7th, to JUNE 26th, 1949

NEWTON — HAYTOR — WIDECOMBE-IN-THE-MOOR

MONDAYS, TUESDAYS, THURSDAYS & FRIDAYS / SUNDAYS

	a.m.	a.m.	a.m.	p.m.	p.m.	p.m.	p.m.	p.m.	p.m.		a.m.	p.m.	p.m.	p.m.	p.m.
Widecombe ... (dep.)															
Haytor		9 30	11 10	1 45	5 0		8 30				10 40	1 45	5 0	8 0	
Ilsington		9 40	11 20	1 55	5 7		8 37				10 50	1 52	5 10	8 7	
Liverton	9 20	9 50	11 30	2 5	5 15	5 3	8 45				10 58	2 0	5 20	8 15	
Exeter Cross	9 25	9 55	11 35	2 10	5 18	5 40	8 50				11 2	2 5	5 25	8 20	
Heathfield	9 30			11 40	2 15		5 45	8 55			11 7	2 10	5 30	8 25	
Teigngrace	9 35			11 45	2 20		5 50	9 0			11 12	2 15	5 35	8 30	
Newton Abbot (arr.)	9 48	10 10	11 58	2 33	5 28	6 0	9 10				11 25	2 28	5 48	8 43	

	a.m.	a.m.	a.m.	p.m.	p.m.	p.m.	p.m.	p.m.	p.m.	p.m.	a.m.	p.m.	p.m.	p.m.	p.m.
Newton Abbot (dep.)		10 30	11 55	12 5	2 45	3 25	5 10	5 35	7 0	9 50	11 30	2 45	6 0	8 50	9 30
Teigngrace		10 40	12 5			3 33	5 20		7 10	9 58	11 40	2 55	6 8	9 0	9 40
Heathfield		10 45	12 10			3 37	5 25		7 15	10 2	11 45	3 0	6 12	9 5	9 45
Exeter Cross		10 48	12 13		2 55	3 40	5 28		7 18	10 5	11 48	3 3	6 15	9 8	9 48
Liverton		10 52	12 20	12 22	3 0	3 45	5 33	5 50	7 23	10 10	11 55	3 10	6 20	9 15	9 55
Ilsington		11 0		12 30	3 8			5 58	7 30		12 5	3 20	6 30		10 3
Haytor		11 10		12 40	3 20			6 10	7 40		12 15	3 30	6 40		10 15
Widecombe (arr.)															

WEDNESDAYS AND SATURDAYS

	a.m.	a.m.	a.m.	p.m.	p.m.	p.m.	p.m.	p.m.	p.m.	w o	s o	p.m.	p.m.
Widecombe ... (dep.)		9 15			1 30		s o	5 0	6 10	8 15			
Haytor		9 30	11 10		1 45		3 20	5 15	6 25	8 30	8 30		
Ilsington		9 40	11 20	s o	1 55	w o	3 27	s o	5 25			8 37	
Liverton	9 20	9 50	11 30	1 40	2 5	3 15	3 35	4 40	5 35			8 45	
Exeter Cross	9 25	9 55	11 35	1 43	s o	2 10	3 20	3 40	4 45	5 40		8 48	
Heathfield	9 30		11 40		1 45	2 15	3 25	3 45	4 50	5 45		8 53	
Teigngrace	9 35		11 45		1 50	2 20	3 30	3 50	4 55	5 50		8 58	
Newton Abbot (arr.)	9 48	10 10	11 58	2 0	2 0	2 33	3 43	4 3	5 5	6 3		9 10	

	a.m.	a.m.	a.m.	p.m.	p.m.	p.m.	s o	w o	s o	w o	s o	s o		w o	s o
Newton Abbot (dep.)		10 30	11 55	12 5	2 35		2 45	4 15	5 15	5 15	7 0	7 0	9 0	9 15	9 30	9 50	10 0
Teigngrace		10 38	12 5		2 45			4 25	5 25	5 25	7 10	7 10	9 25		9 58	10 10
Heathfield		10 43	12 10		2 50			4 30	5 30	5 30	7 15	7 15	9 30		10 2	10 15
Exeter Cross		10 46	12 15		2 53	s o		4 33	5 33	5 33	7 18	7 18	9 33		10 5	10 18
Liverton		10 52	12 20	12 22	3 0	3 0		4 40	5 40	5 40	7 25	7 25	9 38		10 10	10 23
Ilsington		11 0		12 30		3 8	3 8		5 48	5 48	7 33	7 33		9 55		10 30
Haytor	8 50	11 10		12 40		3 20	3 20		5 55	5 55	7 45	7 45		10 5		10 40
Widecombe (arr.)	9 10			1 0			3 35			6 10		8 0		10 20	

s o—Saturdays only. w o—Wednesdays only.

J. POTTER & SONS, Ltd.

TOR GARAGE — HAYTOR — Newton Abbot

Phone—Haytor 233

Wotton Limited, Printers, Newton Abbot

Timetable leaflet for Spring period 7th March to 26th June 1949

Chapter Five : I heard it on Potter's bus

Widecombe-in-the-Moor is known the world over.   On the second Tuesday in September thousands of people head for the small Dartmoor village, lured by the tales of Uncle Tom Cobley, his companions and Tom Pearce's old grey mare.   The ballad had resulted in Widecombe being an essential part of a visit to Dartmoor for many tourists and no day was busier than Widecombe Fair day.   From early morning, vehicles would stream over the moorland roads and deposit visitors in the midst of the village.

For the "Tor Bus" Widecombe Fair has been described as the annual "harvest".   Every available bus would be pressed into service and yet more passengers than the entire fleet could handle would present themselves for a ride to Widecombe.   Devon General buses and drivers would be hired for the day and in pre-war years Gaytons of Ashburton would take over operation of the Bovey Tracey services for the day in order to give further assistance.   Potter's were authorised to operate journeys to Widecombe from all trains arriving at Bovey Tracey Station between 10 a.m. and 6.30 p.m. on Widecombe Fair day and to run return journeys to meet traffic requirments.

The number of passengers travelling was enormous.   For example in 1935 it was estimated that 900 passengers were carried both to and from Widecombe.   Former member of staff, Fred Pady, recalls that in his day Bert Frost would take the money and issue tickets, leaving the drivers to go to and fro.   Bert took £500 in one day which, at a fare of three shillings return, represents over 3,000 passengers.   One vehicle did nine return trips to Widecombe that day.

Ilsington Flower Show also brought crowds and Fred Pady, the mechanic, would drive, with Bert Frost taking the fares.   From the early days of Potter's buses local theatrical events had brought extra traffic.   The point-to-point races also resulted in welcome additional revenue.   The latter has been referred to in a previous chapter.   The sheep-dog trials at Haytor were also popular and there is a story of Bert Frost having ninety people on the forty-seater Sentinel, sitting on each others laps and cramming the gangway.   Just before reaching the trials two policemen were spotted and the overload had to make a quick exit through the rear emergency door to avoid being apprehended by "the law".

On another occasion it had not been possible to use a large vehicle on the Wednesday afternoon service from Newton Abbot, as was usually the practice.   A 29-seater had to be operated on the departure on which both shoppers and schoolchildren were carried.   This resulted in a considerable overload, so the twenty or so scholars were asked to "budge-up" on the back seats. They sat on each others knees and generally squashed in. This left the other seats for the adults. However, a Devon General inspector saw the overcrowding and objected to the bus leaving with such numbers on. Dark threats were made of reporting the firm. "Right then, you children, jump off if you please" was shouted. The youngsters recognized what they had to do in the situation, got off and disappeared round the corner of the Market Place. The bus departed round the one-way system to arrive at the first stop by the Bradley Hotel to find all the pupils waiting to get back on again. Safely out of sight, they climbed on and the bus went on its way with everyone on board happy.

At other times Devon General staff were instrumental in ensuring that "Tor Bus" passengers caught the last bus home at night. The phone would go, at the Devon General office in Newton Abbot, and there would a message from Torquay that Ilsington folk could not reach Newton in time for the half past ten "Tor Bus". Inspector Bishop would kindly come out of the office and say to Potter's driver "You have got to hang on for one of our buses to come up from Torquay – there are five people wanting to go to Ilsington". Departure would be delayed until the party got to Newton and they were all accounted for.

Throughout the life of the "Tor Bus" service drivers would undertake jobs for villagers. Prescriptions would be dropped off at the chemists on the way into town and then collected on the return journey for delivery to the patient. The drivers would regularly be stopped by a villager running out and asking them to do "this bit of shopping for me". It was important that when drivers bought items for people they went to the right shop. Just any old supplier would not do. Some would only have sausages from one butcher. Others must have their cheese from Churchwards. Woe betide the man who shopped in the wrong place and when several people wanted items brought home there would be a lot of tramping about from shop to shop. On one occasion the driver was nowhere to be seen at departure time and it was a quarter of an hour after the appointed time when he finally appeared. "Sorry we are late leaving", he announced, "I have been choosing wallpaper for Mrs So-and-so". Nobody minded in the least. For those travelling on the bus it was a chance to "have a natter". Conversations would start "Have you heard.....?". Every day when villagers were telling each other bits of gossip they would say "I heard it on Potter's bus".

Private party outings were undertaken. Apart from jobs originating in the home villages of Haytor, Ilsington and Liverton, much work was done for organisations in Bovey Tracey and Newton Abbot. Pub customers in Bovey used the "Tor Bus" for their outings, as did the Salvation Army in Newton Abbot, the latter always requesting that Bert Frost drove them. Liverton Football Club were regulars and hotels in Torquay hired the firm to transport French students staying in the town. There were also occasional journeys to places such as Bristol, providing duplicate vehicles for the long-distance coach services of Associated Motorways.

Excursion trips from the villages to the moors, coast or special events were occasionally advertised. The story of one such outing sums up the individual way in which the business ran. One family was asked if they wanted to go on a trip to Bigbury-on-Sea. They said yes and it was arranged that they would be picked up at their gate. At the appointed time the "Tor Bus" duly arrived, but the family were greeted with the question "what have you got buckets and spades for?". "Because we are off to the seaside" they replied. "Oh, no" was the response, "we have changed our mind". Nothing daunted, they got on and the coach was driven round the village, stopping each time a pedestrian was seen. They would be invited to go on a trip. "Where to?" was the reply. "Oh, up over and back along, I reckon". When a satisfactory load had been achieved, the party set off, eventually stopping at Yelverton. Everyone, including a highly pregnant lady, got off and had a game of football, the bus having to be moved each time the ball went under it. They then had tea and in the evening the party arrived back home, all declaring that it had been a wonderful day.

On another occasion the Sunday morning bus came back down through Liverton and at the bottom of the village only two people were left on board. They were going to Blackpool. "Are you in a hurry?" the driver asked. When they said that there was no particular rush to get home they were asked whether they would mind if the driver did a quick job for his sister. They agreed that he could and off he went, leaving them sitting in the bus. Eventually after some forty or forty-five minutes he emerged, having put up shelving for his relative. "Ever so good of you to wait", he said, "it will save me coming back".

The Potter brothers could be a bit fierce with staff. There was an occasion when one of the brothers, shirt sleeves rolled up and arm resting on a bus, was berating a driver for some misdemeanour. Meanwhile, another member of the staff, seeing a chance for some fun, connected leads to the vehicle and put an electric charge through. Mr Potter stopped his conversation half way through a sentence, leaped away and said "this bus is live. For goodness sake go and sort it out". No more was heard about the supposed crime.

Most of the thousands of passengers who used the service with any degree of regularity over the years knew Hubert Henry Frost, always known as Bert. This gentle, well-liked man walked up from his home at Trumpeter Cottages, Ilsington, each morning to start a days work driving a "Tor Bus" or one of the lorries. Quietly confident, rarely smiling but always good humoured, he covered the best part of two million miles at the wheel of the buses on the narrow hilly roads. His service to the travelling public spanned well over thirty years, until he retired on Maundy Thursday, 1962. In the early days he drove with one passenger, "usually a pretty girl", beside him on the driver's seat, which was just big enough for two. The road between Exeter Cross and Widecombe was narrow and twisting but the firm's buses were rarely involved in accidents. Bert recalled that although he had never had an accident, he could not say that nobody had ever driven into him. In fact, hardly a day passed without him having had a fright somewhere along this part of the route. He could remember being beaten by the weather on only one occasion, during the winter of 1946-47. On occasions when the road through Teigngrace was flooded he would drive up to the water, stop the bus, scratch his head and wonder whether he should go through. Invariably, he got it right.

During the summer quite a few visitors would travel on the buses, often to Haytor or Widecombe. As he coaxed the heavily loaded bus up the steep hill into Ilsington, Bert Frost would stand up in the driver's seat, head nearly touching the roof, and gripping the wheel he would rock back and forth "to lighten the load and help the old bus". As the final corner was rounded into the village there would be a round of applause from the passengers. He also lived up to the "Tor Bus" motto "never leave anyone behind". He would say before he left Newton Abbot "where is Mrs. So-and-so? We brought 'er in this morning and she hasn't come back since. We must hang on for 'er". And the bus would wait a quarter of an hour or more for her to arrive.

One passenger did manage to beat the system and get left behind. Leslie Manley tells how his Aunt Alice went to Newton on the bus in the early days but got "yapping" (talking) to folk in the town. Time went on and on and she found she had missed the bus home. Nothing for it but to walk, together with her young nephew who she had brought in. However, she did not take the direct road home, she followed the exact route that the bus had taken on the way in, even walking from Drumbridge up to Heathfield, where the bus turned, then retracing her steps to Drumbridge and so on home!

Bert Frost not only followed the motto "never leave anyone behind", he also observed the rule "always room for one more". There is the story that in the days when he drove the Dodge bus, dubbed the "pigeon basket" by the Staffordshire potters, there were a lot of people waiting for the last bus out from Newton. "The seating was all took up, so they squeezed in more by some sitting on others. They then squeezed all up through the gangway and when that was full some leaned in over the wings and others got on the steps leading up to the roof luggage rack".

A frequent problem was the inability of many city drivers to reverse in the narrow country lanes and occasionally the "Tor Bus" staff would have to get out of their bus and back the visitor's car into a gateway for them so that the bus could pass.

William Arthur (Bill) Baty was another who drove the "Tor Bus". He started work for J. Potter & Sons in about 1942. He was a regular driver, along with Bert Frost, on the Newton Abbot service. The bus would be stopped anywhere along the route to pick up or drop passengers and on market day (Wednesday) the driver would jump out and help with the various cargoes, such as rabbits and chickens, that people would be taking in to sell for a few shillings. The service in from Widecombe would be well loaded, one particular character, Dennis Nosworthy, would send a couple of suitcases full of rabbits which he had caught during the week. The driver would stop the bus at the Market and unload these items, let the passengers off, then spend a lot of his time in town running errands for people who wanted him to collect something from a shop or go and pay a bill somewhere.

Duplicate buses were often needed to cope with passenger numbers on the Widecombe service. Here 40-seater Sentinel LOD 974 is loaded for Widecombe, with Leyland Cub AUO 712 ready to provide relief as far as Haytor.

29-seater Bedford, HFJ 575, in Newton Abbot Bus Station on a short working to Liverton. The "Tor Bus" time table was mounted on a board which is seen just in front of the vehicle. (Alan D. Broughall)

MTA 554, another Bedford OB, in Newton Abbot Bus Station.

AEC Regal ODV 376 had an unusual body by Metalcraft. It was really too wide and long for the narrow, twisting roads traversed on the "Tor Bus" routes and was sold after two years to a South Wales operator, in whose service it is seen.

VME 479 was eight years old when it was bought by J. Potter & Sons from Valliant of London. It was an AEC with a 33-seater body by Gurney Nutting. (R. Marshall)

Seen outside the Tor Garage, Haytor are two Bedfords, SUO 113, an SB model and HFJ 575, an OB.   (R.C. Sambourne)

SUO 113 was the only vehicle to have a cream flash and to carry a "P" insignia.   (Alan D. Broughall)

Burlingham bodied AEC WTT 352 pulls out of Newton Abbot Bus Station on a service journey to Widecombe.

Standing in the door of the Tor Garage is Sid Brinicombe, in later years a director of J. Potter & Sons Ltd. WTT 352 is passing through on service to Newton Abbot.

Sentinel LOD 974, as posed when new for a manufacturer's catalogue photographed presumably in Shrewsbury.

The highlight of every weekday for Bill Baty's son (also Bill) was the first bus from Newton in the morning. This carried the daily newspapers, all neatly rolled up with a piece of gummed paper on which was the name of the house to which it had to be delivered. When the bus arrived at the garage young Bill would get on and assist dad with the papers. As the bus continued round Haytor Vale his father would fling papers out of his open window and young Bill would throw his to the nearside. Sometimes they would land near the door of the house but, quite often, they would lodge in a bush, or if it was wet, in a puddle, especially if the houses were close together when the necessity of delivering to the right premises was at the expense of accuracy. All this was done, of course, at normal speed and without stopping. Inevitably there was the odd complaint and the eyesight of the deliverers would come under question. Bill Baty, junior, remembers that Sid Potter was at one time interested in flying and took lessons at Exeter. He never got a licence but if he had, perhaps they would have been delivering papers from a Tiger Moth.

Ron Coaker, who was mechanic at the time, would sometimes take the bus round the little circuit from the garage to Haytor and back, so that the driver could have a break. The service buses were generally the Leyland Cubs, AUO 712 and AUO 713. Jack Guest, Charlie New and sometimes Les Edworthy, who was the regular taxi driver, would also take part in these general frolics. Walter Gigg and a chap who came out of the army, Hugh Johns, were also employed at the time.

Young Bill was given a job at Tor Garage at the same time as his father. Sid Potter agreed that he could help Ron Coaker in the garage and be general factotum cleaning taxis and buses, at a wage of fifteen shillings a week. He was then fifteen years old. He soon learned to drive the buses and was able to reverse them into the garage in a remarkably tight formation. His favourite was the forward control Leyland Cub, OD 8628. That, to him, was a proper bus. On reaching the age of seventeen he began to drive taxis, the Austin 18hp CTT 425 and the Austin Sixteen EXN 319. At that time he was enlisted in the Home Guard and at one briefing he was informed that in the event of transport being required Potter's buses would be commandeered and that he would be one of the drivers. He did mention (albeit not too loudly) that he was not old enough to drive a bus carrying passengers but was told that under wartime regulations it was in order. Shortly after he was required to drive BOD 841 to Scorriton, carrying some of his platoon for an exercise. He recollects "I felt ten feet tall and needed to be, because the clutch on BOD required the strength of a Goliath!".

As has been noted in an earlier chapter Mary Jane Potter, wife of the founder, was a woman of some determination who played an important part in the early years. Much of what was achieved was due to her care in handling money. Life in the Potter household has been recalled by the very first employee, Leslie Manley. He lived at Liverton and in the summer of May, 1921, he helped Mary Jane, who had a stall at an event in a field near the Star Inn. He fetched buckets of water to heat for the tea, carried the lemonade bottles and generally made himself useful. Mrs. Potter knew his mother and at the end of the afternoon said to him "You had better come and work for father and me when you leave school". In the July, at the age of thirteen years and five months, he was given an exemption certificate and allowed to leave school. He would liked to have been a carpenter but there were no openings and he did not fancy going to work at Bovey Pottery, where he felt sure he would get "Potter's Rot" from the dust. So, he started work for the family at a rate of five shillings a week for a twelve-hour day, six days a week, with just Sundays off. In addition he got three meals a day, with tea, doughcake or bread and cream plus a bible reading mid-morning.

John and Mary Jane Potter rented a meadow from the Stover Estate and on this they kept three cows. They also had pigs and Mary Jane looked after the shop. After a while Mary Jane said to Leslie "it is about time we got you down to milking". However, Leslie had been forewarned by a friend, Bill Rogers, who had told him not to get stuck with that job. They needed milking twice a day, seven days a week and his life would not be his own. So Leslie did not make a good job of it and Mary Jane told him they would never make a milker of him. To which he thought "No, I'm sure you won't!".

He did all the jobs around the house – churning the butter by hand, preparing potatoes, making junket. This meant that whenever the shop bell went "tinkle, tinkle", Mary Jane could go and serve and Leslie could carry on with the job in hand. He would also make potato cake but if he was seen putting some of the currants in his mouth, Mary Jane would tell him sharply "I didn't send you down there for that purpose". He also got into trouble when weighing out goods. Winifred Mary Tapper, with whom he had been at school, came in for 7 lb. of potatoes. As Leslie lifted the box to let them run into the scoop they overflowed and the scale went down bump. Before the extra could be put back in the box Mary Jane, who was in the next room making dough for apple dumplings, heard the bang and thinking he was giving extra to his school friend, rushed in and pushed him out the way. "I buy everything by weight" she said "and I sell it that way, too". Protests that it was an accident went unheard.

Leslie drove the last journey undertaken by the horse-drawn wagonette before it was replaced by the Model "T" Ford motor. A local family had lost their farm in a fire and were moving away. They were taken to the station to catch a train. It is said that at the fire the farmer was the happiest man there. He was flat out and full of cider.

Although Mary Jane was very careful with the money, this was very necessary in those early days. All spare cash was put in a big box up in the bedroom, with leather bags holding half-crowns, florins, shillings, etc. Although her sons thought the money should be in the bank – interest would be one halfpenny per month for each pound, they argued – Mary Jane was happier knowing exactly where it was.

In 1922 Leslie Manley knew that he would have to ask for more money, but did not look forward to the occasion. Mary Jane always took the cash to pay him from the till. There was a big drawer that sloped towards the back and she would open it, reach in, take out one half-crown, then another. One night Leslie said "I am sorry Mrs Potter but I must have more money". The response was predictable. "Oh, my dear soul, us can't afford to pay you no more". "Well in that case" she was told "I shan't be coming Monday morning, I am going to work at Bovey Pottery".

"You can't do that" said Mary Jane, "Mrs Saunders is coming in to do the washing". Blow Mrs. Saunders, thought Leslie. Every Monday he skimmed the milk in up to five pans, then heated the water for the washing, keeping the boiler full and carrying in coal in the scuttle. He left the job but looks back on it as some of the happiest times of his life.

NEWTON ABBOT — HAYTOR — WIDECOMBE

TOR BUS SERVICE — TABLE **117**

MONDAY, TUESDAY, THURSDAY & FRIDAY | WEDS. and SATS.

	a.m.	a.m.	n'n	p.m.	p.m.	p.m.	p.m.	p.m.	p.m.		a.m.	a.m.	a.m.	n'n	p.m.	p.m.	p.m.
Newton Abbot	850	1030	12 0	245	415	510	545	715	9 45	.....	850	1030	12 0	235	245	4 15
Teigngrace	858	1038	1210	255	425	520	555	725	9 55	.....	858	1038	1210	245	.....	4 25
Heathfield	9†0	1043	1215	3 0	430	525	6 0	730	10 0	.....	9†0	1043	1215	250	.....	4 30
Exeter Cross	9 2	1046	1218	3 3	433	528	6 3	733	10 3	.....	9 2	1046	1218	255	255	4S33
Liverton	9 5	1052	1225	3 8	438	533	6 8	740	1010	.....	9 5	1052	1225	.....	3 0	4S38
Ilsington	913	11 0	1233	315	445	.....	615	748	.....	.....	913	11 0	1233	.....	3 7	.....
Haytor	925	11 8	1245	323	455	.....	625	8 0	.....	850	925	11 8	1245	.....	315	.....
Widecombe	.....	.....	.....	.....	.....	.....	.....	.....	.....	910	.....	.....	1 5	.....	328	.....

WEDNESDAY and SATURDAY—continued | SUNDAY

	p.m.	W	S	W	p.m.	S	S	p.m.	W	S	a.m.	p.m.	p.m.	p.m.	p.m.	
Newton Abbot	415	5 0	515	545	7 15	715	920	9 30	10 0	10 0	1130	245	550	850	9 30	.....
Teigngrace	.....	510	525	555	7 25	.....	930	.....	1010	1010	1140	255	6 0	9 0	9 40	.....
Heathfield	.....	515	530	6 0	7 30	.....	935	.....	1015	1015	1145	3 0	6 5	9 5	9 45	.....
Exeter Cross	425	518	533	6 3	7 33	.....	940	9 40	.....	1018	1148	3 3	610	9 8	9 48	.....
Liverton	430	525	540	6 8	7 40	.....	.....	9 45	.....	1025	1155	310	617	915	9 55	.....
Ilsington	.....	438	.....	548	615	7W48	735	.....	9 55	.....	1033	12 5	318	625	.....	10 3	.....
Haytor	.....	445	.....	558	625	7W58	743	.....	10 0	.....	1040	1215	330	635	.....	1015	.....
Widecombe	.....	458	.....	.....	.....	.....	758	.....	1020	.....	.....	.....	.....	.....	.....

MONDAY, TUESDAY, THURSDAY & FRIDAY | WEDS. and SATS.

	a.m.	a.m.	a.m.	p.m.	p.m.	p.m.	p.m.	p.m.		a.m.	a.m.	a.m.	a.m.		S	S
Widecombe	.....	.....	.....	.....	.....	.....	.....	.....		.....	9 15	.....	.....		.....	.....
Haytor	810	9 30	1110	145	325	515	.....	815		810	.....	9 30	1110		.....	.....
Ilsington	817	9 37	1117	155	332	522	.....	822		817	.....	9 40	1120		.....	.....
Liverton	825	9 45	1125	2 5	340	530	535	830		825	915	9 50	1130		140	.....
Exeter Cross	828	9 48	1128	2 8	343	533	540	833		828	918	9 55	1133		143	.....
Heathfield	833	9 53	1135	215	348	.....	545	838		833	925	.....	1138		.....	145
Teigngrace	838	9 58	1140	220	353	.....	550	843		838	930	.....	1143		.....	150
Newton Abbot	848	1010	1153	233	4 3	543	6 0	855		848	945	10 8	1155		2 0	2 0

WEDNESDAY and SATURDAY—continued | SUNDAY

	p.m.	p.m.	p.m.	W	S	W	S	W	S	p.m.	a.m.	p.m.	p.m.	p.m.	
Widecombe	.....	130	.....	330	.....	.....	5 0	5 0	.....	850	.....	.....	.....	.....	.....
Haytor	.....	145	.....	345	.....	.....	515	515	.....	6 0	815	.....	1040	145	5 0	8 0
Ilsington	.....	155	.....	352	.....	.....	522	522	.....	6 7	822	.....	1047	155	5 7	8 7
Liverton	.....	2 5	.....	357	.....	440	530	530	.....	615	830	.....	1055	2 5	515	815
Exeter Cross	.....	2 8	3 0	4 0	.....	443	533	533	535	623	833	.....	1058	2 8	518	818
Heathfield	.....	215	3 5	.....	435	448	.....	540	540	630	838	.....	11 5	215	525	825
Teigngrace	.....	220	310	.....	440	453	.....	545	545	635	843	.....	1110	220	530	830
Newton Abbot	233	323	410	453	5 5	543	558	558	648	855	.....	1125	233	545	845

†—Time at Heathfield Cross.   S—Saturday.   W—Wednesday.

Tor Bus timetable as shown in the Newton Abbot ABC for April 1951.

J. Potter & Sons Ltd., of Tor Garage, Haytor, Newton Abbot, Devon.

H.1421.—(672)—Stage: Between Widecombe-in-the-Moor and Newton Abbot.

(1) To introduce interavailability of tickets with Devon General Omnibus and Touring Co. Ltd. (Application H.436), between Heathfield and Newton Abbot only and vice versa.

(2) To introduce a 12-journey weekly ticket for adult passengers only for a six day week at a charge of eight times the single fare. Forward journey to be completed by 9 a.m. and return journey not to be made before 12 noon.

(3) To co-ordinate those fares over common sections of route with Devon General Omnibus and Touring Co. Ltd. and to revise the fares over the remainder of the route, in accordance with the following schedule:—

Cheap Day Returns

Newton Abbot—Widecombe	3/9
Newton Abbot—Haytor Rocks .. :	3/-
Newton Abbot—Haytor (Moorland Hotel)	2/8
Newton Abbot—Haytor Vale	2/7

S—Single. R—Return.

Main fare table (single fares from each stage, as read):

From Widecombe	From Harefoot Cross	From Hemsworthy	From Haytor Rocks	From Haytor (Moorland Hotel) / Tor Garage	From Lewthorn Cross	From Ilsington Church / Silverbrook
6d.	3d.	4d.	2½d.	3d.	2½d.	3½d.
8d.	7d.	5d.	5d.	4d.	4½d.	6d.
11d.	8d.	9d.	6½d.	4½d.	7d.	7d.
1/-	11d.	1/-	7d.	6d.	8d.	7½d.
1/4	1/-	1/4	10d.	8d.	11d.	10d.
1/6	1/1	1/6	1/1	8d.	1/-	1/-
1/8	1/4	1/7	1/2	9d.	1/1	1/1
1/9	1/5	1/9	1/4	1/1	1/5	1/6
1/9	1/6	1/10	1/6	1/1	1/5	2/2
1/11	1/7	2/2	1/8	1/2	1/6	2/3
2/-	1/8	2/4	1/9	1/6	1/6	2/3
2/2	1/10	2/10	1/11	1/7	1/7	2/4
2/4	1/10	2/11	1/10	1/8	1/7	2/4
2/6	1/11	3/-	2/-	1/8	1/7	
2/6	2/-	3/11	2/-	1/8	1/7	
2/8	2/4	3/11				
2/8	2/4					
S	R	S R	S R	S R	S R	S R

Lower section:

From Liverton Mill	From Liverton Kiosk	From Blackpool	From Exeter Cross (Summerhill)	From Heathfield	From Teigngrace	From School Lane	From Mount Pleasant	From Teign Grace Lane / Wain Lane
2d.	3½d.	2½d.	3d.	3d.	2d.	2d.	2d.	2d.
3½d.	4d.	7d.	3½d.	3½d.	2½d.	3d.	3d.	Newton Abbot
4d.	6d.	8d.	5d.	4d.	4d.	4d.	5d.	
7d.	8d.	10d.	5½d.	5d.	5d.	6d.		
9d.	9d.	10d.	10d.	7d.	1/-	10d.		
10d.	11d.	10d.	10d.	9d.				
10d.	11d.		1/4					
11d.	11d.		1/4					
11d.			1/4					
S	R	S	S	R	R	R	R	R

Application to revise fares and introduce interavailability of tickets with Devon General published in Notices & Proceedings for 11th October 1956.

40

Chapter Six : The Final Years

With the number of bus passengers declining as private car ownership grew, the building of a new housing estate at Heathfield resulted in a major confrontation between J. Potter & Sons Ltd and Devon General. The site was adjacent to the point at which Potter's buses emerged from the lane leading from Teigngrace on to the main Exeter–Plymouth road. There was also a frequent Devon General service between Newton Abbot and Bovey Tracey which was not permitted to carry Heathfield passengers to and from Newton Abbot. Both operators needed the extra traffic that an estimated population of over six hundred would bring, as did British Rail with a station at Heathfield, where the Newton Abbot–Moretonhampstead trains connected with the Teign Valley branch to and from Exeter.

Devon General proposed to introduce timings at Heathfield on all journeys in each direction, thus becoming the major operator serving the Heathfield housing estate. This was opposed by Potters, who applied to run a new service between Liverton, Heathfield and Bovey Tracey, against opposition from Devon General. Both applications were opposed by British Rail, Western Region, on the grounds that it already provided a service between Newton Abbot, Heathfield and Bovey Tracey. Supporting both bus operators, but favouring neither, were Newton Abbot Rural District Council and Bovey Tracey Parish Council.

At the public enquiry the Chairman of the Traffic Commissioners, Mr S.W. Nelson, said that although he agreed that the existing service to Heathfield was inadequate in the light of housing development, he suggested that the two bus companies should seek an amicable agreement to share the service so that Potters should not be driven out of business. Discussions ensued as a result of which an agreement was reached whereby common fares and interavailable tickets were introduced on common sections of route and the previous restrictions on Devon General picking up and setting down at Heathfield for Newton Abbot were withdrawn. J. Potter & Sons withdrew their application for a Liverton–Heathfield–Bovey Tracey service and Devon General surrendered their licence for the Newton Abbot–Bovey Tracey–Widecombe service (No.14) leaving the "Tor Bus" to cater for traffic to and from Haytor and Widecombe. The Traffic Commissioners accepted the agreements reached between the two bus operators and the various changes were enacted.

During the summer of 1957 an AEC Reliance joined the "Tor Bus" fleet, this being medium-weight and underfloor-engined with a five-speed gearbox and air braking system. It carried a slightly different livery, the window pillars being red and the three main places served – Newton, Haytor, Widecombe – appeared on the roof sides in gold lettering. This vehicle superceded a petrol-engined Bedford, bought new in 1955, which though giving a smooth, quiet ride was expensive to run at a time when operating costs were rising rapidly and passenger numbers were falling. The fleet was now down to five buses and coaches – three Bedford OB model, one Bedford SB and the AEC. They were all used on all types of work, although the AEC was the main service bus and it was also used to carry the guests at Muriel Potter's wedding with Max Bunclark.

In the autumn of 1958 the Devon County Council opened a new Secondary School at Ashburton and transferred to it chidren living in the Bovey Tracey, Heathfield, Ilsington and Liverton areas. Contracts for the daily conveyance of pupils were put out to tender and J. Potter & Sons Ltd. succeeded in their bid for three routes:-

- Ashburton and Bovey Tracey (Route A), 33 seater
- Ashburton and Bovey Tracey (Route B), 29 seater
- Ashburton and Ilsington, 29 seater.

The revenue was £2. 15s. 0d. a day for each of the three vehicles but these gains were partly offset by the cancellation of the Ilsington–Newton Abbot contract, for which a 26-seater had been specified at a daily payment of £2. 13s. 0d. The Secondary Modern pupils who had used it now went to Ashburton and those attending the Grammar School at Newton Abbot were given season tickets for the "Tor Bus" public service.

Within a year the Bovey Tracey A and B routes to and from Ashburton school had been changed so that both vehicles followed the same route. This allowed boys and girls to be conveyed on separate vehicles. No reason is given for this in official records but it is known that on one school contract operated by the firm some high spirits resulted in one girl's head going through the rear window.

During 1960 a new type of vehicle was purchased. This was an eleven seater Commer minicoach and it was used to convey local schoolchildren to and from Ilsington School, as well as staff to and from Hawkmoor Sanatorium.

Although fewer people were using the buses the "Tor Bus" staff did not depart from their standard of service. The winter of 1962-63 brought severe weather conditions, similar to 1946-47. Ice and snow made driving hazardous and it was so cold that diesel froze in the fuel pipes of vehicles. After a heavy snowfall the A38 was quiet and deserted. No one expected the bus to run through Blackpool to take the schoolchildren into Newton Abbot. However, at 9.15 a.m. a horn was heard and there crawling up the lane was the "Tor Bus" with pupils on board. It slithered up the main road to reach Heathfield, where children were dispatched to the houses of regular passengers to tell that the bus was getting through. In the evening the bus was there to bring home both schoolchildren and workers. "We'll get through".

In these later years the original ticket punch system had been superceded by Insert Setright machines. Season and weekly tickets were available at discounts.   Exchange tickets were issued when accepting Devon General return tickets under the interavailability arrangements.   The Newton Abbot terminus was also removed from its traditional stand in the Market Place to a bay in the Bus Station.

However, the decline in passengers continued as more people turned to private transport.   The loss was particularly noticeable among visitors to the moor and this had an adverse effect on bus service revenue.   Efforts to improve the position by increasing fares had not worked and in an average week buses carried 1,500 to 2,000 passengers.   This was not nearly enough to cover costs. Although the contracts and private hire work was profitable there was not a sufficient margin to subsidize the losses on the service.

The Directors of the company, having reviewed the position, decided with sadness that all operations should cease after 31st August, 1963.   They were sorry to withdraw a service which had served the local community well for over forty years but it was apparent that private car ownership was continuing to increase rapidly.   The licence for the Newton Abbot–Haytor–Widecombe service was surrendered and the school contracts terminated.   The six buses and coaches in the fleet were disposed of and four drivers made redundant. The Commer minicoach passed to Wilfred Potter's daughter, Muriel Bunclark, who continued to convey local schoolchildren as well as Hawkmoor Sanatorium staff.

With the cessation of operations by J. Potter & Sons Ltd, there passed a well-known operator who ran interesting vehicles on a challenging but picturesque route.   It was subject to dramatic variations in weather over the seasons and sometimes within a few hours of one day.   The business had progressed from horse-drawn wagonette to modern vehicles, always smartly turned out.   Although the main places served had only small populations the "Tor Bus" provided an excellent level of service and was very much part of the local scene.   In the words of Dick Wills, the local historian of Ilsington, "it was a great service to the community and always done in a friendly manner".

"Never leave anyone behind"

"Always room for one more"

"We'll get through"

From the GATEWAY of DARTMOOR . . .

. . . on to DARTMOOR !

By the . . .   —Also Luxury Coaches for Hire

TOR BUS SERVICE

SUMMER—Commencing JUNE 10th, 1962 until further notice

NEWTON — HAYTOR — WIDECOMBE-IN-THE-MOOR

DEPARTURE POINT NEWTON ABBOT BUS STATION

Almost the end: Summer timings from 10th June 1962

MONDAYS, TUESDAYS, THURSDAY & FRIDAYS | SUNDAYS

	a.m.	a.m.	a.m.	a.m.	p.m.	p.m.	p.m.	p.m.	p.m. SH	p.m.	p.m.	p.m.	a.m.	a.m. SH	a.m.	p.m.	p.m.	p.m.
Widecombe ... (dep.)					1 30		4 15		5 06	15			1 30	4 45	8 15			
Haytor (Moorland Hotel)	7 38	10 9	30	1115	1 45	3 30	4 30		5 15	6 30	8 20	10 35.1	4 55	08	30			
Ilsington	7 10	8 17.9	40	1122	1 55	3 37	4 37		5 25	6 37	8 27	1045.1	5 5	108	40			
Liverton	7 18	8 25 9	47.	1130	2 2	3 45	4 45		5 32	6 45	8 35	1052.2	2 5	178	47			
Blackpool	7 21	8 28.9	50		2 5	3 48					8 38	1055.2	5 5	208	50			
Exeter Cross	7 23	8 30.9	52	1133	2 7	3 50	4 48		5 35.6	48	8 40	1057.2	7 15	228	52			
Heathfield	7 28	8 35	10 0	1138	2 15	3 55	4 53			6 51	8 45	11	1 52	15.5	30	9 0		
Teigngrace	7 33	8 40	10 5	1143	2 20	4 0	4 58			6 55	8 50	1110.2	20 5	35	9 5			
Newton Abbot (arr.)	7 41	8 48	1015	1155	2 33	4 13	5 5		5 48.7	3	9	3	1123.2	33 5	45	9 15		

	a.m.	a.m.	a.m.	a.m.	p.m.	p.m.	p.m.	p.m.	p.m.	p.m.	p.m.	a.m. SH	a.m.	p.m.	p.m.	p.m.	p.m.
Newton Abbot (dep.)	7 45	8 50	1030	12 0	2 45	4 15	5 15	5 50	7 10			10 0	1130	2 45	5 50	9 45		
Teigngrace	7 53	8 58	1038	1210	2 55	4 25	5 25	6 0	7 20			1010	1140.2	55 6	09	55		
Heathfield	7 58	9c 2	1043	1215	3 0	4 30	5 30	6 5	7 25			1015	1145.3	06	510	0		
Exeter Cross	8 1	9 5	1046	1218	3 3	4 33	5 33	6 8	7 28			1018	1148.3	36	810	3		
Blackpool		9 8	1048	1220	3 5	4 35	5 35	6 10	7 30			1020	1150.3	56	1010	5		
Liverton	8 6	9 13	1055	1225	3 10	4 40	5 40	6 15	7 35			1025	1153.3	106	1510	10		
Ilsington	8 14	9 20	11 3	1233	3 18	4 48	5 48	6 23	7 43				12 53	18.6	23	1018		
Haytor (Moorland Hotel)		9 28	1113	1243	3 28	4 58	5 58	6 35	7 50			1215	3 30	6 30	1025			
Widecombe (arr.)			1128	1 0	3 43		6 10					1235	3 45					

c—Calls Heathfield Cross only.

SH—Operates School Holidays—July 26th to September 5th.

WEDNESDAYS

	a.m.	a.m.	a.m.	a.m. SH	p.m.	p.m.	p.m.	p.m.	p.m.	p.m.	p.m.	p.m. SH
Widecombe ... (dep.)			9 15		1 30		3 30		5 06	15		
Haytor (Moorland Hotel)	7 38	10 9	30	1115	1 45	3 45		5 15	6 30		8 20	
Ilsington	7 10	8 17.9	40	1122	1 55	3 52		5 25	6 37		8 27	
Liverton	7 18	8 25 9	47.	1130	2 2	3 45	4 0	5 32	6 45		8 35	
Blackpool	7 21	8 28.9	50		2 5	3 48					8 38	
Exeter Cross	7 23	8 30.9	52	1133	2 7	3 50	4 3	5 35.6	48		8 40	
Heathfield	7 28	8 35	10 0	1138	2 15	3 55			6 51		8 45	
Teigngrace	7 33	8 40	10 5	1143	2 20	4 0			6 55		8 50	
Newton Abbot (arr.)	7 41	8 48	1015	1155	2 33	4 13	4 13	5 48.7	3		9 3	

	a.m.	a.m.	a.m.	a.m.	p.m.	p.m.	p.m.	p.m.	p.m.	p.m.	p.m.	p.m. SH
Newton Abbot (dep.)	7 45	8 50	1030	12 0	2 45	3 0	4 15	4 15	5 15	5 50	7 10	10 0
Teigngrace	7 53	8 58	1038	1210		3 10	4 25		5 25	6 0	7 20	1010
Heathfield	7 58	9c 2	1043	1215		3 15	4 30		5 30	6 5	7 25	1015
Exeter Cross	8 1	9 5	1046	1218		3 18		4 25	5 33	6 8	7 28	1018
Blackpool		9 8	1048	1220		3 20			5 35	6 10	7 30	1020
Liverton	8 6	9 13	1055	1225	3 0	3 25		4 28	5 40	6 15	7 35	1025
Ilsington	8 14	9 20	11 3	1233	3 8			4 36	5 48	6 23	7 43	1033
Haytor (Moorland Hotel)		9 28	1113	1243	3 15			4 43	5 58	6 35	7 50	1040
Widecombe (arr.)			1128	1 0	3 28			4 56	6 10			1055

c—Calls Heath Cross only.

SH—Operates School Holidays—July 26th to September 5th.

SATURDAYS

	a.m.	a.m.	a.m.	a.m.	a.m.	p.m.	p.m.	p.m.	p.m.	p.m.	p.m.	p.m.	p.m.	p.m.
Widecombe ... (dep.)			9 15			1 30		5 0		8 5				
Haytor (Moorland Hotel)	7 38	10 9	30		1135	1 45	3 30	5 15	6 08	20				
Ilsington	7 10	8 17.9	40		1142	1 52	3 37	5 22	6 78	27				
Liverton	7 18	8 25 9	47.		1149	1 35	2 23	4 54	4 05	32.6	158	35		
Blackpool	7 21	8 28.9	50.			2 5	53	48	6 188	38				
Exeter Cross	7 23	8 30.9	52			1152	38	2 73	50 4	43.5	35.6	208	40	
Heathfield	7 28	8 35	10 0	1045		1 45	2 15	3 55	4 48.	6 25	8 45			
Teigngrace	7 33	8 40	10 5	1050		1 50	2 20	4 0	4 53.	6 30	8 50			
Newton Abbot (arr.)	7 41	8 48	1015		11 0	12 52	3	2 30 4	13 5	3 5	45.6	40 9	3	

	a.m.	a.m.	a.m.	a.m.	a.m.	p.m.	p.m.	p.m.	p.m.	p.m.	p.m.	p.m.
Newton Abbot (dep.)	7 45	8 50	1030	1030	12 0	1210	2 45	4 15	4 15	5 05	5 07	10 10 0
Teigngrace	7 53	8 58	1038		1210		2 55	4 25		5 20	6 07	20 1010
Heathfield	7c58	9c 2	1043		1215		3 0	4 30		5 25	6 57	25 1015
Exeter Cross	8 1	9 5		1040	1218		3 3	4 33	4 25	5 28.	6 87	28 1018
Blackpool		9 8		1042	1220		3 5	4 35		5 30	6 107	30 1020
Liverton	8 6	9 13		1045	1225	1225	3 10	4 38	4 30.5	35.6	157	35 1025
Ilsington	8 14	9 20		1053		1233	3 18		4 38.5	42	7 43	1033.
Haytor (Moorland Hotel)		9 28		11 0		1245	3 28		4 45.5	50.	7 50	1040
Widecombe ... (arr.)				1115		1 0			4 58		8 3	1055.

—Calls Heathfield Cross only.

J. POTTER & SONS, Ltd.

TOR GARAGE — HAYTOR — Newton Abbot

Phone—Haytor 233

Wetton Limited Printers, Newton Abbot   Price 1d.

44

Chapter Seven : Postscript

The decision of J. Potter & Sons Ltd. to cease operations meant that although Heathfield would continue to be served by a frequent Devon General service and Widecombe was linked to Ashburton and Newton Abbot by Beard's bus, there were a number of settlements which would lose their entire public transport service. These were Haytor, Ilsington, Liverton and Teigngrace.

The week after the closure of the "Tor Bus" service had been announced it became apparent that a Government Bill which had just been passed could possibly have saved the service and the four villages from isolation if anything had been known about it. Under the Local Government (Financial Provisions) Act local authorities were able to use up to a penny rate to subsidize bus services. In Newton Abbot Rural District this would have produced £2,850 a year, which some perceived would have been enough to keep the "Tor Bus" service going. However, the firm made it clear that it was too late now. Even if they had known about this, it would not have made any difference.

A committee of Newton Abbot Rural District Council discussed the closure but it is unlikely that the councillors knew about the possibility of subsidy. They decided to ask Devon General to take over the service but Mr L.J. Crook, Traffic Manager, said he knew nothing about the subsidy and that they already ran a high number of unremunerative services in the Newton Abbot district and were not anxious to take on any more.

However, there was a reprieve for the villagers when a former "Tor Bus" driver, R.D. Woolley, of Pine Springs, Haccombe applied to provide a replacement service and also to operate between Haccombe and Newton Abbot. He planned to run the buses jointly with Mr V. English, also of Haccombe. They began at the start of September, 1963, so there was no break in the service. The two partners were offered terminal facilities at Newton Abbot bus station by Devon General.

Mr English looked after maintenance and financial matters while Mr. Woolley drove the forty-one seater Foden coach named "Betty". They ran as far as Haytor on Mondays, Tuesdays and Thursdays and to Widecombe on Wednesdays, Fridays and Saturdays. There were four trips a day on the shorter journey and six a day on the longer one. The name "Dartmoor Bus Company" was used.

The new operator did not find it easy to maintain the service and by the summer of 1964 operations were irregular. Trade inevitably dropped off and one Tuesday in May of that year schoolchildren and business people who travelled to work by bus found themselves stranded when they tried to get home in the evening. People who had come to work on the bus had to hire taxis or arrange for lifts home. There was no bus service on Wednesday and things looked bad for the villagers. Mr Dick Wills, a member of Ilsington Parish Council, approached Mr Jim Snell, a Newton Abbot coach operator and former member of "Tor Bus" staff, with a view to Snell's Coaches taking up the service. This was agreed and a temporary licence was granted to continue. However, operations were short-lived as Mr Snell was fully committed with school buses and private hire and found that he had no drivers available for the service.

The third operator within a short time took over. Devon General now stepped into the breach and introduced a new route (No. 23) which left Newton Abbot each Wednesday, Friday and Saturday at 9.15 a.m., 1.45 p.m. and 6.15 p.m., returning from Widecombe at 10.15 a.m., 2.45 p.m. and 7.15 p.m. Villagers were given another chance to get to Newton Abbot and holidaymakers to get to the moors.

From the GATEWAY OF DARTMOOR on to DARTMOOR

By the **TOR BUS SERVICE**
NEWTON — HAYTOR — WIDECOMBE
Services from—Bus Station, Newton Abbot
Time Tables free on receipt of stamped addressed envelope
Proprietors— **J. POTTER and SONS, LTD.**
Depot & Offices— **Tor Garage, Haytor, Newton Abbot**
Phone—HAYTOR 233
Private Hire Service   CARS—20, 26 & 29 SEATER COACHES

THE PEOPLE

"Tor Bus" - Potter family and known staff

John Potter
Mrs Mary Jane Potter

Family:
George Potter
Wilfred Potter
Sidney Potter
Mrs F.A. Potter
Mrs E.M. Potter
Muriel Potter (later Mrs. Bunclark)
Sidney Brinicombe

H.W. (Tiny) Brockway (company secretary)

Bert Frost (driver)
Bill Baty, sen. (driver)
Vic Bowden (driver)
Ron Coaker (fitter,driver)
Les Edworthy (taxi,driver)
Walter Gigg (driver)
Jack Guest (taxi,driver)
Harry Heathman (driver)
Gordon Hole (driver)
Tom Keep (driver)
Tom Leaman (driver)
Harry Newton (driver)
Jack Prouse (driver)
Bill Rowe (driver)
Bill Richards (driver)
Fred Sampson (garage hand)
Robin Retter (driver)
Miss Heather Wise (office)
Mrs Peggy Brinicombe (conductor)
Les Cann (taxi)

Leslie Manley (boy)
Bill Baty, jun. (garage)
Bert Bray (driver)
Miss Grace Cox (driver)
Reg Giles (driver)
Billy Guest (cleaner)
Bill Hatherley (driver)
Hugh Johns (driver)
Reg Hill (fitter)
Harry Kemp (driver)
Charlie New (driver)
Fred Pady (fitter,driver)
Harold Osborne (driver)
Gilbert Roberts (driver)
Harold Retallick (driver)
Jim Snell (driver)
Bill Avery (garage,driver)
Stuart Mogridge (office)
R.D. Woolley

There are no doubt others whose names have not been included but who, nevertheless, were among those who were part of the friendly "Tor Bus" service.

THE VEHICLES

Seating code: B = Bus, C = Coach, followed by number of seats.

J. Potter - J. Potter & Sons - J. Potter & Sons Ltd.

Regn.No.	Make/Model	Body	Seats	Acquired	Wdn
TA 1706	Ford "T" 22hp	Vallance	Lorry/14	Jul.21	ca.27
TT 7388	Graham Dodge	?	B14	Mar.26	ca.33
UO 1659	Dodge	?	B14	Mar.27	Mar.34
DV 244	Dodge	?	B20	Mar.29	ca.36
DV 5596	Dodge	Strachan	B20	Mar.30	Nov.38
OD 6213	Commer Centurion		C20	Jun.33	ca.34
OD 8628	Leyland Cub SKP3	Duple	C26	Mar.34	Dec.49
YT 1118	Maudslay ML4	?	B25	Jan.35	Jan.38
JY 5355	Dennis Ace	Mumford	B20	Mar.35	-.38
AUO 712	Leyland Cub KP3	Mumford	B26	Jul.35	Oct.51
AUO 713	Leyland Cub KP3	Mumford	B26	Jul.35	Sep.50
BOD 841	Dennis Ace	Duple	B20	Aug.36	Mar.49
COD 948	Dennis Pike	Dennis	B20	Aug.39	Aug.53
HFJ 575	Bedford OB	Duple	C29	Aug.47	Jun.62
KTT 492	Bedford OB	Mulliner	B31	Jan.49	Oct.57
LDV 787	Leyland CPO1	Devon C.B.	B31	Apl.50	Aug.55
LOD 974	Sentinel STC4	Beadle	B40	Jul.50	Dec.56
MTA 554	Bedford OB	Duple	C29	Sep.50	Sep.63
ODV 376	AEC Regal IV	Metalcraft	B43	May.53	Apl.55
SUO 113	Bedford SBO	Duple	C38	Apl.55	Sep.63
TTA 72	Bedford SBG	Duple	C38	Jun.55	May.57
WTT 352	AEC Reliance	Burlingham	B45	Jun.57	Sep.63
VME 479	AEC Regal III	Gurney Nutting	C33	May.58	Sep.63
325 GTA	Commer 1500VH	Marshall	C11	Nov.60	Sep.63
ROE 238	Bedford SBG	Duple	C35	Jun.62	Sep.63

Notes:
All vehicles bought new except:-
    YT 1118, previously operated by Robin & Rambler, London, new in 1927
    VME 479 was previously operated by Valliant, London W5, new in 1950
    ROE 238 was previously operated by Stevens, St. Ives, new in 1955

Subsequent owners:-
TA 1706 and DV 244 were both converted to lorries by Potter, last licensed May.37 and Jun.37 respectively.
TT 7388 last licensed to Willesden Scrap Iron Co., London NW1, Sep.35

OD 6213 to Harris, Ipplepen; Irwin, Trebetherick; Wellington, Kingsbridge.
Last licensed to Belgrave Motors, Plymouth (dealer) Dec.51.
LDV 787 to Ward, Wickford, last licensed Oct.61
LOD 974 to Venner, Witheridge; Heard, Hartland (not operated); CDE, Porton
Down (mess hut); preserved.
MTA 554 to Snell, Newton Abbot, last licensed Feb.64
ODV 376 to James, Burry Port; Jenkins, Pontardulais, last licensed Mar.67
SUO 113 to Venner, Witheridge; Down, Ottery St. Mary; Dawlish Coaches,
Dawlish; to caravan.
TTA 72 to Venner, Witheridge; Morse, Veryan.
WTT 352 to M. & M. Kidderminster.
325 GTA to Mrs M. Bunclark, Haytor.
VME 479 to Staverton Contractors, Totnes.

All other vehicles had no subsequent owners.
KTT 492 was last licensed in Oct.57 but the Traffic Commissioners records
show it as withdrawn in Nov.59.

Livery : Maroon, Red and Black.
      OD 6213 - Green.
      YT 1118 - at first blue, then to usual livery

Vehicles of other operators referred to in this book

J. Dart, The Garage, Ilsington

| TT 7389 | Dodge | ? | C14 | Mar.26 | -.31 |
| DV 9233 | Dodge | ? | C14 | May.31 | ca.32 |

Notes:
TT 7389 was known as the "Haytor Coach"
DV 9233 was advertised as the Dart Coach, All-Weather Saloon
Both vehicles bought new. Livery - Unknown

R.D. Woolley (& V. English), Flat 3, Pine Springs, Haccombe.
"The Dartmoor Bus Company"

NPT 903	Foden PVRG6	A.C.B.	C41	Sep.63	May.64
NHY 465	Sentinel SLC4	Beadle	C35	Sep.63	May.64
DUX 945	Bedford OB	Duple	C29	Sep.63	May.64

Previous operators:-
NPT 903 and NHY 465 - Caterer, Tring (NHY465 new to Bristol Co-op in 1951)
DUX 945 - Northmead Coaches, Tadley, new in 1947
Livery - Red, Cream and Black.

O 9800

TOR BUS SERVICE

SINGLE

This ticket is issued subject to the rules & conditions of the Company. Must be shown on demand & is NOT TRANSFERABLE

Williamson, Printer, Ashton

DAY | MONTH | STAGE | SHIL'S | PENCE

A 9800

TOR BUS SERVICE

RETURN

This ticket is issued subject to the rules & conditions of the Company. Must be shown on demand & is NOT TRANSFERABLE

Williamson, Printer, Ashton

DAY | MONTH | STAGE | SHIL'S | PENCE

W 9800

TOR BUS SERVICE

RETURN

This ticket is issued subject to the rules & conditions of the Company. Must be shown on demand & is NOT TRANSFERABLE

Williamson, Printer, Ashton

DAY | MONTH | STAGE | SHIL'S | PENCE

HAYTOR BUS SERVICE

PERIOD TRAVEL TICKET № 155

(not transferable)

Pass Miss
　　　Master
between.................................... and.....................

commences.............................. expires......................

available MONDAYS to FRIDAYS only.

For travel once in each direction only on the days stated, the forward journey must be completed at or before 9.30 a.m. and is available for the return journey after 12 noon only.

This Ticket is not available on Sundays, Bank Holidays, Good Friday, Christmas Day.

Signature of Holder...................................

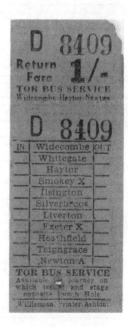

D 8409

Return Fare 1/-

TOR BUS SERVICE
Widecombe Haytor Newton

D 8409

IN		OUT
	Widecombe	
	Whitegate	
	Haytor	
	Smokey X	
	Ilsington	
	Silverbrook	
	Liverton	
	Exeter X	
	Heathfield	
	Teigngrace	
	Newton A	

TOR BUS SERVICE
Available ... journey on which issued and stage opposite Punch Hole
Williamson, Printer, Ashton

Examples of tickets used by Tor Bus - actual size.
Colours are (top row left to right) buff, green, salmon
and (bottom row left to right) old gold, brick red.

TOR BUS SERVICE

Handed In

Conductor's Waybill for _____ day _____ 19 __	Interavailability Tickets _____
	School Tickets _____
Driver's Name _____	Other Tickets _____
	Warrants _____
Conductor's Signature _____	Cashier's Signature _____

MACHINE SUMMARY

CASH PAID IN

£	s.	d.

Machine No.		Passengers or Tickets	Shillings or Cash	Pence or Ex.	Total Passengers	Total Sh'ngs or Cash (½d.)	Total Pence	£	s.	d.
	Closing No.									
	Opening No.									
	Closing No.									
Total	Opening No.									
CREDITS Error Tickets					½d. over pt.	...				

TICKET SUMMARY

Spares in Box	Total No.	Classification	Opening No.	Closing No.	Tickets Used
		SINGLE			
		RETURN			
		EXCHANGE			
		½d. Overprint SINGLE			
		½d. Overprint RETURN			
				Total ...	

Gross Total	...
Less Credits	...
Nett Total	...

Parcel Tickets

Quantity	Op'n'g No.	Closing No.	Used
6d.			
8d.			
1/-			

Time Tables Sold

TOTAL (if not in accordance with Cash slip, reason to be given below)

REPORT

JOURNEY SUMMARY

age No.	Time	Single	Return	Exchange	½d. over pt. Single	½d. over pt. Return	Passengers or Tickets	Shillings or Cash	Pence or Ex.	6d.	Parcels 8d.	1/-	Inspector's Initial	No. of Pass'ng'rs on Board

Example of journey waybill used (late 1950's)